THE BIG BOOK OF
CONSPIRACY THEORIES

Cider Mill Press Book Publishers
"Where good books are ready for press"
PO Box 454
12 Spring Street
Kennebunkport, Maine 04046
Visit us online
cidermillpress.com

Typography: Calluna, Octin Stencil, Futura PT, Silk Remington

Image credits: Pages 15, 16, 18, 33, 37, 41, 59, 62, 71, 74, 87, 104, 133, 139, 143, 156, 171, 178, 191 used under Creative Commons licenses. All other images licensed from Vault Editions.

Printed in Malaysia

1 2 3 4 5 6 7 8 9 0

First Edition

THE BIG BOOK OF
CONSPIRACY THEORIES

HISTORY'S BIGGEST
DELUSIONS & SPECULATIONS
FROM JFK TO AREA 51, THE ILLUMINATI,
9/11, AND THE MOON LANDINGS

TIM RAYBORN

CIDER MILL
PRESS

BOOK
PUBLISHERS
KENNEBUNKPORT, MAINE

CONTENTS

CHAPTER 3: SECRET SOCIETIES

CHAPTER 4: POLITICS

CHAPTER 5: SECRET & MYSTERIOUS LOCATIONS

CHAPTER 6: SCIENTIFIC CONSPIRACIES

INTRODUCTION

WE ALL LOVE A GOOD CONSPIRACY THEORY! No matter who we are, almost everyone at one time or another has entertained the idea that there might be more to a news story or an event than the "official" explanation is letting on. Often, those in power give people good reason to believe that something else is happening behind the scenes, maybe even something sinister.

Conspiracy theories aren't new, as some of the entries in this book show. People have always been suspicious of those in power, or of things that seemed a bit too convenient. But over the last sixty years or so, the number of conspiracy theories has expanded to an absolutely huge collection of everything from those that might just be true, to those that are completely off the wall.

Why are there so many now? A lot of people believe that the assassination of President John F. Kennedy in 1963 changed many people's thinking about just what was happening in the corridors of power and beyond. The strange circumstances around that whole event, plus the assassination of Kennedy's alleged killer, Lee Harvey Oswald, only fired the imaginations of many and led them to believe that there was much more to the story than what they were being told. Several other high-profile assassinations over the next few years (Malcolm X, Robert Kennedy, and Martin Luther King Jr.) only fed that fire. Whispers of US covert actions in other countries and on the home front, the growing opposition to the Vietnam War, the rise of the counterculture and a skeptical young population . . . all of these things fed into the idea that people were being lied to, perhaps on a grand scale. Conspiracy theories became a part of the protest against that abuse of powers.

Maybe such chaotic times required that people try to find ways to connect the dots to make sense of it all. In the decades since, we've been trying ever harder to connect those dots, to make sense of seemingly random and pointless events over which we have no control. The rise of the internet and its echo chambers, where people can reinforce each other's beliefs and exclude outsiders, has only made conspiracy theories more popular.

This book is a collection of some of the most famous and not-so-famous conspiracy theories in that vast array of such tales. These include everything from actual conspiracies (MK-Ultra and Operation Northwoods) to the more famous theories (the moon landings were faked, the Earth is actually flat, and Hitler escaped from Germany) and the more fringe ideas (Australia doesn't exist and Britney Spears is a clone). It's a guide and reference to ideas both funny and frightening. Feel free to dip in and read wherever you like. Just be sure to look over your shoulder from time to time—you never know who might be watching your every move. . . .

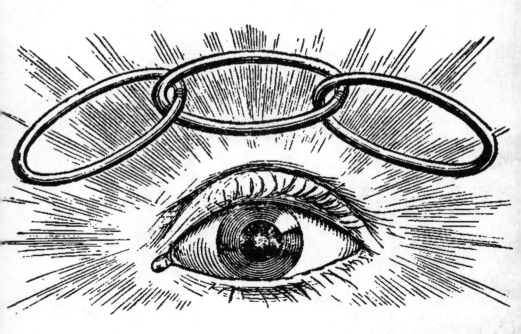

A HISTORY OF THE END OF THE WORLD

CHAPTER 1
HISTORICAL CONSPIRACIES

CONSPIRACY THEORIES ARE BY NO MEANS a modern invention, though thanks to the internet and social media, there are a lot more of them now, and they can spread much wider than ever before, which is frequently a bad thing. But even before this rapid transfer of information, people have long been skeptical of rulers, disasters, and often, the very people who lived among them. Suspicion and superstition can make for tragic companions. This chapter delves into some of the more important conspiracy theories from centuries and decades past to show that a lot of people have held fringe beliefs, no matter what time they lived in.

NERO AND THE BURNING OF ROME

YOU'VE PROBABLY HEARD THE STORY of how, when Rome burned in 64 CE, the insane emperor Nero stood by and fiddled. He was so far gone that he thought it was funny, and decided to do nothing and let his city burn. It's an odd little tale, to be sure, but sorry to say, it has nothing to do with the truth. Bowed instruments like the fiddle didn't find their way into Europe for another 1,000 years, so that detail can be immediately ignored. Okay, some argue, but it might have been another instrument, like a lyre, a harp-like instrument that was very popular at the time and that Nero loved to play.

In fact, Nero fancied himself as quite the poet and musician, even though, by all accounts, he was pretty boring and average. Still, he would make people sit and listen to him for hours, and since he was the emperor, no one could leave, not even for emergencies or bathroom breaks! So, could he have strummed a lyre while his city went up in flames? It's possible, but there are no reports at the time of him doing it.

It seems that he was out of the city, and when he heard about the disaster, he immediately rushed back to Rome and tried to do what he could to help put out the fire and contain it so it didn't spread. He even offered new dwellings to some of those who had lost their homes, which was a kind thing to do.

So, was Nero actually a good guy? Not really, and that's where we get into the conspiracy theory—one of the oldest in this book, in fact. In some of the areas that were damaged by fire, Nero didn't offer to rebuild homes, but simply demolished everything and built a new palace for himself. The fire gave him the opportunity to do some "urban renewal" without having to do a lot of extra work or pay to have intact buildings demolished. He got exactly what he wanted, and some people found it suspicious.

People started whispering that he had ordered the fire to be deliberately set to destroy those buildings, so that he could claim the land for himself. On one hand, he acted like he was very concerned for those

who were left homeless, while on the other, he was already planning a grand new residence for himself. It feels rather like one of those news reports of a sleazy landlord setting fire to his own building to turn out the tenants and collect the insurance money.

Is this what happened? Well, Nero was certainly devious enough to do it, and it seems like some people think he did, even at the time. Did he plan the destruction of that part of Rome and then enforce a conspiracy of silence about it? We might never know for sure, but it's one conspiracy theory that might just have some truth to it.

THE CALENDAR IS OFF
BY SEVERAL CENTURIES

WHAT YEAR IS IT? You might be wrong. At the time of writing, we are (allegedly) living in the early 2020s, but there are some who think that's nonsense. According to believers in the "phantom time hypothesis," we're actually living in the early eighteenth century. But how? Why? Well, it all goes back to the theories of a German writer and researcher, Heribert Illig, and his colleague, Dr. Hans-Ulrich Niemitz.

Illig started investigating some key dates and points in the Early Middle Ages (previously known as the "Dark Ages"), and found what he thought were discrepancies in the time line. He pointed to a lack of much archeological material and findings from this era, the continued use of Roman-style ("Romanesque") architecture right into the Middle Ages (suggesting that the Roman Empire had ended far closer in time to the Middle Ages than previously thought), and a complex calculation

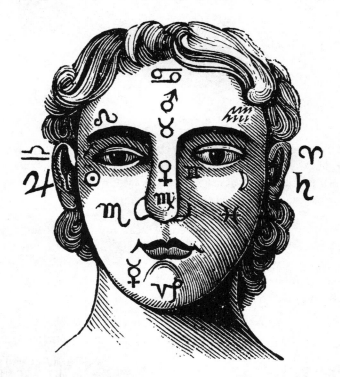

that looked at the Julian and Gregorian calendars. Given that the Julian calendar needed to be revised by 1582, Illig believed that it should have been off by thirteen days, but it was only off by ten or eleven. To him, this meant that there were at least a few "phantom centuries" inserted into the time line. But who would do something like this, and why?

The theory is that the Holy Roman Emperor, Otto III, along with Pope Sylvester II, and maybe the Byzantine Emperor, Constantine VII, conspired to move the time line forward, because Otto wanted to be emperor during the all-important year 1000. Since this was still 297 years away for him, the three agreed to change the time line and dates and pretend that the first millennium was fast approaching. Since the majority of the population was illiterate and had no way of knowing, it would be a simple enough task. Monks and scholars could easily be pressured to stay silent until the new time line had established itself firmly enough in popular belief and the old years were forgotten.

It's a theory that's just strange enough to be true, but it falls apart under closer investigation. Astronomical observances from Europe and the rest of the world discuss eclipses and recurring celestial visitors such as Halley's Comet, which appeared right on schedule throughout those centuries. Independent observations from China (which had no direct contact with Europe) also confirm these time lines. Indeed, the Tang dynasty had its own interactions with the Islamic world in those centuries, completely independent of Europe, which are well recorded. Important historical figures such as Charlemagne, King Alfred the Great, and Muhammad all lived in this so-called nonexistent time, and they are recorded in countless chronicles and stories. The Viking raids in Europe and their trade missions to Byzantium and the Arab world happened then, too, and are again recorded in sources outside of Western Europe. Dendrochronology (dating by tree rings) also proves the existence of these centuries.

So, what at first seems like a weird and even possible conspiracy theory turns out to be just plain wrong and a bit silly. No serious historians who have looked at the evidence have come out in favor of the idea that our time line includes a few extra, nonexistent centuries.

QUEEN ELIZABETH I
WAS SECRETLY A MAN

QUEEN ELIZABETH I ascended to the throne of England in 1558, after several years of political upheaval and social turmoil. Her father, Henry VIII, had torn apart the country in the 1530s by abolishing the Catholic Church and setting up his own independent Church of England. He did this in order to legally divorce his first wife, Katherine of Aragon, and marry his mistress, Anne Boleyn, who was, incidentally, Elizabeth's mother.

After Henry's death, his son, Edward VI, became the king at only nine years old. Edward wanted the new Protestant Church to be England's official religion, but he accomplished little and died at the age of fifteen in 1553. According to the laws of succession, the next of Henry's off-spring in line for the throne was his daughter, Mary. Mary was a devout Catholic, and wasted no time in reestablishing the Catholic religion as England's official faith, and persecuting Protestants who opposed her; hence her nickname, "Bloody Mary." But she was also in poor health, and died in 1558.

When Elizabeth became queen, there might have been a collective sigh of relief that things could stabilize for a while, and indeed they did. She would go on to rule England for nearly forty-five years and establish it as a major European power. But she never did the one thing that so many hoped she would: marry and have children. Dubbed "the Virgin Queen," she would tell her courtiers that she was "married to England," and that would be all they would ever have from her. But why did she do this? Then as now, many people wondered. Some thought she had a string of affairs with noblemen and wanted to keep them private, and may have even given birth to a child or two in secret.

But one conspiracy theory suggests something far more unusual: "Queen Elizabeth" was actually a man. This story goes back to author Bram Stoker, who wrote *Dracula*. While visiting Bisley, an English village, Stoker learned about their legends and traditions. They believed that in 1543, Henry VIII sent eleven-year-old Elizabeth to the village for her own safety during an outbreak of plague. But she had already contracted the plague and died soon after. The villagers panicked about what Henry would do, so they found a boy of her age that looked like her and had him take on the role. Since Henry spent very little time with Elizabeth, he never noticed the switch.

The boy had to assume the role for the rest of his life, and went on to become one of England's greatest monarchs, keeping men away by vowing never to marry. It was the greatest cover-up (literally) in English royal history. Of course, it's an absurd story without a shred of real evidence, though Stoker firmly believed it. It's laced with sexist attitudes—a woman couldn't possibly have accomplished what Elizabeth did—and ignores several key facts. Elizabeth did have many male favorites, and it's unlikely that none of them would have noticed "she" was a man. Even if they were threatened with silence, that kind of hot gossip would have gotten out eventually. Also, King Philip II of Spain considered marrying her, and bribed one of Elizabeth's laundresses to reveal if she was fertile. The laundress reported that she "functioned" normally, meaning that she menstruated. So this odd little speculation can safely be thrown away as an unfounded rumor.

SHAKESPEARE DIDN'T WRITE SHAKESPEARE

WAIT, WHAT? At first, this seems like a very strange claim. We all know that the author of such masterpieces as *Romeo and Juliet*, *Hamlet*, and *King Lear* was a man named William Shakespeare from the English town of Stratford-upon-Avon. He lived in the sixteenth and early seventeenth centuries and created some of the most memorable characters in all of English literature. Generations of students have been taught this and have read (and enjoyed or hated) his plays, and maybe even tried their hand at acting in some of them.

But according to some theories, it's all been a lie. There was an actor named William Shakespeare, yes, but he could barely read or write, and could not possibly have had the education he needed to create such lavishly detailed plays, with their constant mentions of faraway places, Greek and Roman mythology and history, and dozens of other things that make the stories so rich. No, some say, it had to be an educated person, someone with money and the time to sit and write such things.
But who?

One of the current favorite choices is Edward de Vere, the Earl of Oxford. Many believe that he secretly wrote the plays (since it was not considered "proper" for a nobleman to write plays at the time) and allowed Shakespeare to put his name to them, but left hints in his work that pointed to his identity. There's one big problem with this theory: de Vere died in 1604, and Shakespeare was still writing plays in 1613 that mentioned events from the years after 1604.

Another candidate is Christopher Marlowe, the genius young playwright who died after being stabbed over the eye in a tavern fight in 1594. Or did he? Some believe that since he was a known spy, he faked his death to go on working for Queen Elizabeth's government in secret, but still wrote plays, which, he allowed Shakespeare to put his name to.

Another possibility is Sir Francis Bacon, a statesman, scientist, and philosopher who, like Edward de Vere, might have written plays in secret, since they were considered beneath him by his friends. Others have suggested that Queen Elizabeth herself wrote the plays, but like Edward de Vere, she died in the early seventeenth century (1603), unless she somehow lived on in secret, too! In all, more than eighty (!) possible alternate writers have been suggested.

As strange as this theory might seem, it does have support from various actors and others, even though the evidence is thin and the claims are conflicting; the "solid proof" for one possible author often makes it impossible for another author to be the "real" Shakespeare, even though both have supporters claiming theirs is the one.

Some of the playwriting was almost certainly done in collaboration, with actors reading lines and suggesting changes, so in that sense, Shakespeare is not the only author of his plays; he probably made changes that the actors requested. But in fact, no one doubted that Shakespeare wrote his own works until the early nineteenth century; none of his fellow actors and playwrights ever suggested he didn't write his plays. Were they all "in on it" too? Probably not. It's a theory that's interesting at first, but when you examine it more closely, you start seeing the problems, as with so many of these conspiracy theories.

THE SALEM WITCH TRIALS

ONE OF THE MOST INFAMOUS series of incidents in early American history, the Salem witch trials were a kind of horror story, one that has lasted down the centuries and inspired literature, art, and much more. The idea of innocent-seeming citizens living among the New England

Cum privil. Sa.G.M.

Anno.1596.

settlers, who were secretly in league with the Devil, was irresistible then and now. So what really happened in that small Massachusetts town in 1692–1693? As you might expect, rumors, hysteria, and more than a little conspiratorial thinking all came together to create a unique social situation with tragic results.

By the beginning of 1692, Salem was in a bit of a bad state, having endured the effects of a British war with France, economic troubles, and the presence of Reverend Samuel Parris, a minister who was disliked by many in town. Salem had Puritan beliefs, and some soon began to see the town's troubles as something more diabolical. In January 1692, Parris's nine-year-old daughter, Elizabeth, and eleven-year-old niece, Abigail Williams, started to have fits of screaming, throwing things and contorting themselves into odd positions. Along with another girl, Ann Putnam, they soon claimed that three women were responsible: Tituba, the Parrises' Caribbean slave; Sarah Good, a beggar; and Sarah Osborne, an old woman.

The superstitious Salem folk immediately suspected witchcraft, and while the two Sarahs denied any wrongdoing, Tituba confessed, possibly hoping to be spared. After this, accusations began to fly, and people began suspecting witches were everywhere among them, hiding in plain sight. Several more people were brought in for questioning as the investigation expanded beyond Salem to other villages. Rumors of a widespread network of witches began to grow, as the fear fed on itself. Governor William Phips allowed for a special court to be convened, but things began to get out of hand. Soon, over 200 people had been accused, including the governor's own wife. This was apparently enough for him to try to rein things in, and others also realized that this conspiracy theory was becoming ridiculous.

In all, twenty people were executed for being witches, nineteen by hanging, while one was pressed to death with heavy rocks. Those responsible eventually admitted that they had murdered innocent people, and Phips pardoned everyone held in prison on witchcraft charges. The trials were declared unlawful in 1702, but it was not until 1957 that the Commonwealth of Massachusetts officially apologized for the events. It was a good example of how a conspiracy theory can flare up and spread like wildfire, showing how dangerous some fringe beliefs can be.

Historians have said that the fits and other strange behaviors might have been caused by ergot poisoning. Ergot is a fungus that can grow on grains and, if eaten, can cause spasms, hallucinations, and vomiting, all things that the witches' supposed victims experienced. Add to that the depressed economy, a superstitious population, and the ease with which conspiracy theories can spread, and we can see a recipe for an early American tragedy.

THE *TITANIC* DIDN'T ACTUALLY SINK

APRIL 15, 1912, was a terrible day in nautical history. On that day, the *Titanic* struck an iceberg in the North Atlantic and sank, killing at least 1,500 passengers. The ship of which it was said, "Not even God himself could sink her," went down with surprising ease in a few hours. It was a tragedy that would never be forgotten—the 1997 movie based on that event went on to become one of the highest-grossing films in history.

But what if the ship didn't sink? At first, that seems like an absurd thing to say. Of course it did; there were countless eyewitnesses and the wreck itself has been discovered at the bottom of the ocean. Yes, it's true that a ship went down after hitting the iceberg. But, say some conspiracy theorists, it wasn't the *Titanic*. The *Titanic* was actually swapped out with another, older ship that was passed off as the *Titanic* and was the one that went to a watery grave instead.

According to this theory, an earlier ship, the *Olympic*, was the actual ship that sank. It had been involved in an accident at sea (crashing into a military vessel) that had caused considerable damage to it. Being a money pit, its owners decided to make a secret switch. They would swap names, and the *Olympic* would now be called the *Titanic*, and vice versa. The damaged ship would sail as the *Titanic*, and sometime on or after its trip to New York, it would have a convenient "accident" and be so damaged that it couldn't be repaired. The owners could then collect insurance for their "new" ship that was actually the *Olympic* in secret.

The only problem was, they didn't count on this still-damaged ship hitting an iceberg and sinking. A more sinister version of the conspiracy theory says that financier and banker J. P. Morgan had enemies on board the ship that he wanted eliminated, and he was willing to sacrifice hundreds of innocent people to do it.

Proponents of this theory say that the *Titanic* was not allowed a public examination before its maiden voyage, and the reason for this was that those behind this plan feared such an inspection would reveal that the ship was really the *Olympic*. Some theorists claim that there was a difference in the number of windows between the *Titanic* while it was being built and in the final version that sailed, and this proves it was a different ship.

Those who have investigated these claims say that they can easily be explained. The ships were not identical, and the *Titanic* had modifications (to its café and restaurant, for example) from earlier models that were seen on the ship's maiden voyage. The number of windows was also changed, and both ships had the same number by 1912. There are also problems with the insurance amount claimed for the ship, which there shouldn't have been if the ships were swapped.

So, in all likelihood, the *Titanic* went down in the cold ocean waters that night. But might Morgan have wanted some of the people on the ship dead? It's not impossible, and that story might just be the tip of the iceberg.

THE BURNING OF THE REICHSTAG

ON THE NIGHT of February 27, 1933, a fire broke out in the building that housed the Reichstag (the German parliament). This dramatic event would become one of the most important of the 1930s, setting in motion the full rise of the Nazis to power in Germany and leading to World War II. And the Nazis themselves would promote conspiracy theories about the event and use it to consolidate their power.

It was discovered that the fire was caused by arson, and Reich Chancellor Adolf Hitler immediately blamed communists, whom he said were plotting to overthrow the government. Tensions had been building in Germany for some years as the Great Depression swept the world, and there was much dissatisfaction among the people. President Paul von Hindenburg feared that communists allied with the Soviet Union would use the growing unrest to topple his government, so he reluctantly allied himself with the Nazi party and named Hitler his chancellor, hoping that, together, they could fend off the communist threat. It proved to be a terrible mistake.

Once in power, the Nazis immediately began working to solidify their political gains and choke off any opposition. And they concocted a quick way to do so. The Reichstag fire caused the equivalent of over a million dollars in damage before it was put out, but the political damage was far greater. Police arrested a young Dutch man named Marinus van der Lubbe, a worker who favored the communists. He allegedly confessed to the crime and was later executed by beheading.

Hitler was able to convince Hindenburg to invoke emergency powers to give the police more authority to search, question, and arrest anyone who might be suspicious or sympathetic to van der Lubbe. It allowed the Nazis to work up their vision of a police state and eliminate rivals. When Hindenburg died in 1934, Hitler was able to take complete control of the country.

It was all very convenient for the Nazis, but who actually set the fire? Historians still aren't quite certain. Some believe that van der Lubbe did indeed start the fire, but that he was convinced to do it by Nazis posing as communist agents. Others think that Nazi conspirators did it themselves and used van der Lubbe as an easy person to blame. It gave them exactly the results that they wanted, and it would have been a clever way of not only getting that power, but being able to paint the communists as violent enemies of the nation.

We might never know who set the fire, or by whom it was planned, but it's certain that Hitler and the Nazis used it to their best advantage, made up stories, and increased fear and paranoia among the population. It was a Nazi conspiracy theory that worked all too well.

PEARL HARBOR WAS
ALLOWED TO HAPPEN

THE ATTACK ON PEARL HARBOR in Hawaii on December 7, 1941, was the "date that will live in infamy," as President Franklin D. Roosevelt called it. A surprise Japanese attack devastated the US naval base, destroying several ships. It signaled the entrance of the United States into World War II, both in the Pacific and Europe. Up until that point, the United States had mostly tried to stay out of the conflict that had been raging in Europe since 1939, while also watching the increasing Japanese aggression in the Pacific Theater.

The bombing was presented to the American public as a shocking and unprovoked attack, and led to quick resolutions to declare war against both Japan and Germany. A public that had previously been reluctant to get involved in foreign wars had suddenly witnessed a conflict that came too close for comfort. If the Japanese could attack Hawaii, would they aim for the West Coast of the United States next? And for some conspiracy theorists, this reversal of thinking is at the root of the problem: What better way to get an unwilling American population to change its mind and support a war than to bring it right to the people, to show the urgency of fighting it?

The theory is that Roosevelt had long been in favor of entering the war, seeing the threat that both Germany and Japan posed, but was prevented from doing so by both those in the government and by the opinion of the general public. He had already done deals with Britain to shore up their defenses against German attacks, adding to the war effort without actually entering it. While he insisted that no American boys would be sent to fight in a foreign war, it was obvious to him that Germany and Japan needed to be stopped. Theorists suggest that he increased tensions with Japan on purpose in 1940 and 1941, with embargoes and economic sanctions, in a deliberate attempt to provoke Japan into a desperate move. His plan worked. Growing increasingly desperate, Japan decided to launch a surprise attack on American naval forces in retaliation. Roosevelt knew it was coming, so the theory goes, and prevented the intelligence from reaching the US Navy in time, and so was able to justify taking the United States into war.

But those who have investigated the details (including newer, declassified findings) find that this is simply not what happened. Yes, the United States did try sanctions and embargoes against Japan in an attempt to check its growing power and increased militarism, but there is no evidence that this was to provoke a war, or that the United States learned of an impending attack in the days before December 7. Indeed, the thinking at the time (including Roosevelt's) was that if Japan tried anything in retaliation for the embargoes, it would be some kind of skirmish against American bases in the Philippines. The idea that Japan would sail a fleet thousands of miles across the Pacific to attack Hawaii was unthinkable. Whatever Roosevelt's feelings about the ongoing global war, he didn't resort to manipulation and sacrificing American lives to enter into it.

HITLER ESCAPED FROM GERMANY

ON APRIL 30, 1945, in the last days of World War II, Adolf Hitler took his own life in the Führerbunker in Berlin, determined that he would never be captured alive. He and his new wife (and longtime companion), Eva Braun, killed themselves as the Soviet army was closing in. Braun took a cyanide capsule, and Hitler shot himself in the head. Afterwards the bodies were burned to prevent them from being found. This is the standard narrative for what happened as the war came to an end in Europe, but the idea that Hitler may have survived and escaped, having faked his own death, was irresistible to both conspiracy theorists and to his remaining followers, who wanted to believe that the fight was not yet over.

The idea that Hitler survived came not from secretive theorists locked in their rooms, dreaming up elaborate plots, but instead from one of the world's best-known political figures: Joseph Stalin. At a postwar conference in June 1945, when asked about Hitler's body, Stalin said that Hitler was alive and either living in Spain or in Argentina. Of course, this caused an uproar, and quite a few people repeated his words. Newspapers began reporting stories (that were really Soviet propaganda) that the remains of a body alleged to be Hitler's were actually those of a double. Stalin's government was actively trying to sow disinformation at the time, and it became a springboard for all kinds of conspiracy theories.

It was known that various Nazi officials had indeed escaped to South America, some taking refuge in Argentina under the dictator Juan Perón. Perón has been called many things, including a fascist, but his own brand of leadership was particular to Latin America, and it seems that he wanted the technology and innovation that refugee German scientists could bring, just as the United States did. In any case, since there were many German Nazis fleeing to Argentina, it wasn't a big stretch to suspect that Hitler and Braun might be among them. Some believe that Hitler escaped via submarine and lived quietly in exile in the Northwest of the country, near the Chilean border, dying in 1962.

Various sightings of him were reported over the years (both in Europe and in South America), and in 1955, a man named Phillip Citroen, who claimed to be an ex-member of the SS, said that Hitler first had hidden in Colombia and then moved to Argentina in the mid-1950s. A declassified document about him shows a grainy photo of Citroen sitting next to a man who does indeed resemble Hitler, which he claimed was taken in 1954. The man went by the name "Adolf Schüttelmayor," and it was said that the Nazis in Colombia revered him, but the CIA decided it wasn't worth looking into. Other theories suggest that Hitler lived until 1984, that he was secretly in contact with the Vatican, that he even took refuge at a secret base in Antarctica (which was later destroyed; see the Secret & Mysterious Locations chapter), that he is living on the dark side of the moon, and so on. Yes, they get increasingly sillier as they go!

The reality is that a few years ago, a team of forensic scientists was able to examine fragments of a jawbone and teeth in Russia's possession, which were said to have come from the charred remains of Hitler's body. The team made comparisons of these teeth with surviving dental records for Hitler, and found that they were a match. Teeth don't lie. There is no doubt now that Hitler did die in the last days of the war, probably by his own hand.

THE PROTOCOLS OF THE ELDERS OF ZION

THIS HORRID BOOK is the most notorious anti-Semitic work of modern times, and was widely circulated from 1903 on. It first appeared in serial form in a Russian newspaper, but later was bound into a book and distributed in Europe and elsewhere by 1905. It was read with interest in Germany and other countries and translated into many languages. In a series of twenty-four chapters, or "protocols," it lays out its "evidence" for a vast, worldwide Jewish conspiracy which would allow Jews to assume control of everything.

According to the book, the Jews are secretly controlling world economies, manipulating what people read and hear, and trying to stir up wars and conflicts, all with the goal of consolidating their power. The book claims to be an exposé, bringing light to these shadowy and sinister activities by revealing this group's secret meetings. The work was proven to be a fraud by 1921. An article in the London *Times* showed that portions of it were copied from the *Dialogue in Hell Between Machiavelli and Montesquieu*, a French political satire written in 1864 by Maurice Joly, which had nothing to do with the Jews. Other sections were copied from additional books, and reworked.

Of course, this didn't stop those who wanted to believe in it from believing in it. Henry Ford, founder of the Ford Motor Company, published articles based on the *Protocols* in his newspaper, *The Dearborn Independent*. He was later praised by both Hitler and Himmler for his "commitment" to the truth. Naturally, the Nazis used the book to full advantage, publishing something like twenty-three editions between 1919 and 1939, and even using it in schools. Hitler continued to promote the lie that "Jewish-Bolshevists" were secretly plotting to take over the world, and only the Nazis could stop them.

As early as 1935, a Swiss court declared the work to be a fraud, and fined the Nazi sympathizers who were circulating it in Switzerland. In the 1960s, the US Senate called the *Protocols* false, and said that the writing was "gibberish."

Unfortunately, exposing this book as fraudulent propaganda has not eliminated it from the minds of those who wish to believe its lies. Some neo-Nazi groups believe that the *Protocols* are true, and will regularly quote from them and try to offer "proofs" that the book is still accurate, over 100 years after its publication. The damage that this book did to Jewish populations in Europe was immense and appalling. It was the culmination of years, if not centuries, of anti-Semitic belief, condensed into one book and set loose on a gullible readership that was all too eager to believe its outlandish claims.

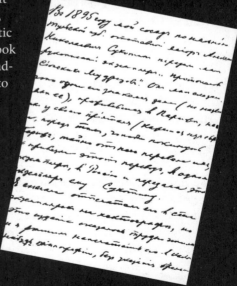

OTHER ANTI-SEMITIC CONSPIRACY THEORIES IN HISTORY

UNFORTUNATELY, the Jews have been subjected to an astonishing number of conspiracy theories and accused of countless plots over the centuries. These accusations have come about largely in Europe, and are due to Christian prejudices about the nature of Jesus. Jews have been accused of being "Christ killers" going back almost 2,000 years, especially after Christianity began to separate itself from Judaism. By the close of the first century, Christianity became less a sect of Jewish belief and more a new religion on its own, and it wasn't long before some believers turned on the religion that had inspired theirs.

By the Middle Ages, anti-Semitic conspiracy theories were well established in Europe. In addition to being guilty of deicide, Jews were accused, openly or quietly, of all manner of things, including:

The blood libel: One of the most persistent and horrid of conspiracy theories, this claimed that Jews ritually murdered Christian children in order to drink their blood, in mockery of Christ's "This is my blood" speech given at the Last Supper. Such children were usually tortured first, and sometimes crucified, before their blood was caught in a bowl and drunk by the Jews at the ritual. This grotesque fiction was common enough that it circulated in legends in several European countries in the thirteenth and fourteenth centuries.

Desecration of the Host: It was said that the Host, the wafers eaten at the Catholic Mass, was sometimes stolen by Jews and ritually desecrated in their own rituals. The penalty for anyone found guilty of this action was death. Of course, it never happened, but that didn't stop trials from going forward.

Crusade violence: During the period of the Crusades (beginning in 1096), those who were going to the Holy Land to try to take it back from Muslim control would sometimes get sidetracked and attack Jewish communities instead. Why go all the way to Jerusalem to fight God's "enemies," they reasoned, when those same enemies were already close to home? Despite Church efforts to stop the violence, it continued for centuries.

The black death: When the bubonic plague struck Europe in the late 1340s, there was a widespread belief that Jews had somehow conspired to poison wells and other water and food sources. Jews accused of this crime were tortured until they "confessed." The fact that Jews themselves also got sick and died didn't convince many people that they were innocent; if anything, people saw it as divine punishment for supposed Jewish sins. Pogroms and persecutions sprang up spontaneously, despite Pope Clement VI trying to dispel the violence by issuing two papal bulls (official statements) in 1348. Clement condemned the attacks and said that anyone who believed the plague was caused by Jews had been deceived by Satan, but the delusions of crowds and mob violence could not be stopped so easily.

Persecutions of the Jews waxed and waned at various times in the Middle Ages, often fueled by ridiculous conspiracy theories. None of the accusations against them had a shred of truth, but that didn't stop horrific rumors and beliefs from spreading rapidly, and sometime erupting into deadly violence with tragic outcomes.

HOLOCAUST DENIAL

HOLOCAUST DENIAL is among the ugliest and worst of all conspiracy theories. It might seem that this belief is not even worth discussing in a book like this. Some conspiracy theories are strange, some are bizarre, some are even funny and fun, but denial of one of the worst atrocities of the twentieth century is none of those things. It's a stark reminder that lies and misconceptions can have real-world consequences. Conspiracy theories helped in part to lead to the Holocaust, and subsequent conspiracy theories about it never happening dishonor the memories of those who suffered through it and died. So, it's in the spirit of truthtelling that this entry is here.

To put it simply, those who believe in this theory think that Nazi Germany's systematic mass murder of Jews never happened, or has been grossly exaggerated. They hold to flimsy ideas, an occasional inconsistency, and what they call a "lack of real evidence." Most are neo-Nazis, or have sympathies with those beliefs. They often try to put themselves forward as serious scholars, holding conferences and writing papers with footnotes (which just cite other Holocaust denial papers), but there is nothing serious about them.

The theory holds that the Allies, in cooperation with Jews, made up stories about Nazi atrocities to further demonize Germany after the war, and to pave the way for the creation of the state of Israel. They fashioned tall tales, fabricated evidence, and sold this mass murder to the world as something that actually happened, when it didn't.

Holocaust denial is rooted in anti-Semitism, and it comes from the same thoughts that produced the *Protocols* and various other conspiracy theories about the Jews over many centuries. At its root, it says that this horrific story was made up, because it was the only way for Jews to gain enough sympathy in the world to establish a nation of their own.

The lies of Holocaust deniers are easily debunked. During the Nuremberg trials after the war, prosecutors produced more than 3,000 documents and pieces of evidence showing that a systematic plan for Jewish extermination was a central part of Nazi policy. Many of these were Nazi authored and were captured by the Allies before they could be burned. It's true that Hitler never signed off personally on ordering mass extermination, but this is because he had done that once before (for the mentally ill) and it had greatly damaged his popularity and image and forced him to backtrack. He would not make the same mistake again. Further, no war criminal put on trial ever declared that these crimes did not occur. They simply went back to that old defense that they were only "following orders."

Holocaust deniers are not interested in true history. They have an anti-Semitic agenda, one that was held by those with similar views who came before them in centuries past. Their so-called "proofs" are nonsense, and they do not deserve serious attention. Of all the conspiracy theories in the world, this one perhaps most deserves to disappear forever.

CHAPTER 2

ASSASSINATIONS & DISAPPEARANCES

THE ASSASSINATION OF A PUBLIC FIGURE can leave people reeling. Whether the victim is a beloved or hated politician, movie star, music entertainer, or anyone else, when someone dies violently, it often leaves people wanting to find an explanation for why. This is especially true if the person in question is influential or is changing the culture in some way that not everyone likes. Then it seems more likely that something else might be behind the killing.

We're naturally bothered by things we can't solve. And this is even truer with disappearances. When someone or a group of someones goes missing, it can be frustrating if we don't figure out why. In both cases, conspiracy theories can move in and take over pretty quickly, as, once again, people try to connect dots that might not otherwise be possible to connect. This chapter looks at some of the world's most famous assassinations, and a few vanishings that have left investigators baffled. Is there something more to these cases than we've been told?

ABRAHAM LINCOLN'S ASSASSINATION

IT'S AN AMERICAN TRAGEDY that just about everyone knows. In a shocking twist that came near the end of the Civil War, President Abraham Lincoln was assassinated on April 14, 1865, while attending a play, "Our American Cousin," at Ford's Theatre. It was a "shot heard 'round the world" which shocked the nation. And yet, it was not completely surprising, given how much hatred was simmering in the country. General Lee had surrendered only days earlier, on April 9, and it was obvious that the Confederacy was doomed. So, there were plenty of people with enough animosity and resentment to want Lincoln dead. But the question was, who did it? Here are some likely answers, and a few less likely conspiracy theories:

The lone gunman: John Wilkes Booth (more on him in the next entry) acted alone. Booth was an actor and a Confederate loyalist who was furious about the outcome of the war. At first, he wanted to kidnap Lincoln, but when things started getting too complicated for that, he resorted to killing him instead.

A Confederate plot: This idea was popular right after the assassination, and it made sense. The idea of killing the president did not seem at all unlikely, especially since Union plans to try to do the same thing to the Confederate president, Jefferson Davis, were later discovered. It's possible that Judah Benjamin, the Confederate Secretary of State, was involved in a plot to kill Lincoln. He fled to England after the war and died in 1884.

The vice president: Again, at the time, there were suspicions about Andrew Johnson, Lincoln's vice president. Several hours before shooting Lincoln, Booth went to visit Johnson at his residence in a hotel. He even left a note stating that he didn't wish to disturb him. Did they know each other? Did they conspire with each other? Or was Booth intending to shoot Johnson as well? Lincoln's widow, Mary Todd Lincoln, always believed that Johnson was involved in a plot to kill her husband.

A group of European bankers: A group of wealthy and powerful bankers led by the infamous Rothschilds ordered Lincoln to be killed, because his financial policies were at odds with their own. He favored policies that would have led to America being independent of European

bank loans and would have ruined their investments and speculations. The Rothschilds wanted control of the American economy, and Lincoln was getting in the way.

The Roman Catholic Church: Charles Chiniquy, and ex-priest with an ax to grind with the Catholic Church, insisted from 1886 onward that the Church, with the approval of the pope, had authorized the assassination. When Lincoln was a lawyer, he had defended Chiniquy in 1856 against a slander charge brought by a friend of a powerful bishop. Lincoln organized a settlement, one that Chiniquy thought humiliated the Church. So, they were out for revenge, and instructed Jesuits to train assassins for the job. Since Rome also opposed Lincoln's policies, it was only natural that they would want him dead.

The Illuminati: Probably, since they've done everything else in history, apparently.

Aliens: Probably not, but who knows?

JOHN WILKES BOOTH
WASN'T KILLED

HISTORY RECORDS THAT actor John Wilkes Booth was a Confederate sympathizer who assassinated Abraham Lincoln in Ford's Theatre on April 14, 1865, as the American Civil War was ending and a fragile peace was being restored. Booth fled from the theater and at some point seems to have injured his leg. He managed to evade capture until April 26, when he was hiding out in a barn with Union Army soldiers on his tail. Caught and surrounded, he refused to come out, so his pursuers set the barn on fire to flush him out. Sergeant Boston Corbett caught sight of Booth in the barn through a large crack in the wooden-board wall. He claimed that Booth raised his gun to fire at him, so he shot and hit Booth, seriously wounding him in the neck.

Booth was dragged from the burning barn, but the Union soldiers realized that he was going to die. They tried to make him comfortable, and about two hours after he was shot, he died, unable to breathe. It was a scandal, because the soldiers had orders to bring in Booth alive; in fact, they were ordered not to shoot. Corbett was immediately court-martialed, though most people in the Northern states saw him as a hero.

But as the story was investigated, contradictions started popping up. Others who were there said that events didn't happen the way Corbett claimed. Some of his fellow soldiers said that they never saw him fire his gun; his gun was never inspected to see if it had been shot. The owner of the farm with the barn, along with his son, said that Booth never raised his gun to Corbett, so Corbett couldn't have acted in self-defense. The soldiers were under strict orders to bring in Booth alive for questioning, and they failed in the one thing they were supposed to do. So if Booth didn't threaten to shoot Corbett, and Corbett never raised his gun, what really happened?

We'll never know, but as we've seen, some people believe that there was a conspiracy to assassinate Lincoln. In other words, Booth didn't act alone. He was part of a larger group made up of businessmen and even Union politicians who wanted Lincoln dead. While Booth was given the task, he proved to be incompetent, so it was taken away from him and assigned to a man named J. W. Boyd, a Confederate soldier who looked very much like Booth. Furious about this, Booth went ahead and carried out the murder anyway.

The conspirators knew that he had to be eliminated so that he wouldn't reveal their secrets, and they sent Boyd and others to take him out. It was Boyd who was actually hiding out in the barn when Union soldiers arrived. He was shot, whether by Corbett or someone else. The government learned of this, but decided it was better that Booth be "dead," so they arranged a show trial of Corbett and let him off easy. Booth escaped to England and then possibly went to India, and the government covered up the whole story.

It's an intriguing tale, but other researchers have since discovered proof that Boyd actually died in January 1866, nine months after Booth was shot. So it couldn't have been Boyd in the barn—unless, of course, you think that's part of the conspiracy, too!

JOHN F. KENNEDY'S ASSASSINATION: LEE HARVEY OSWALD

NOVEMBER 22, 1963, was a day that shocked the world. Shortly after 12:00 p.m. in Dallas, as President John F. Kennedy traveled in an open-car motorcade through the city with his wife at his side, shots rang out from an (at first) unknown location. One of the bullets struck Kennedy in the head, fatally wounding him. In the chaos and panic that followed, police were able to arrest a man, Lee Harvey Oswald, and charge him with firing the killing shots. Oswald immediately denied being the assassin and said that he was being set up. Before he could talk more, he was murdered only two days later (more on that in a later entry of this chapter). Needless to say, this was one of the biggest stories of the twentieth century, and has spawned countless conspiracy theories about what really happened. We'll examine some of the scenarios below.

Oswald acted alone: The Warren Commission that investigated the assassination concluded in 1964 that Oswald was the so-called "lone gunman," and that he came up with the idea of shooting Kennedy on his own, fled the scene, was arrested, and then denied his guilt. While this was the official explanation, it didn't sit very well with a lot of people, and still doesn't. Polls still show that almost two-thirds of Americans don't think that Oswald acted alone.

Oswald had help from a second gunman: This is one of the more popular theories, and the main component is the famous "grassy knoll" theory. This knoll was a small hill near the assassination site where many conspiracy theorists have claimed that a second gunman actually fired the killing shot.

Beginning in 1976, the House Select Committee on Assassinations studied the assassination again, and eventually reached the conclusion that Oswald probably did not act alone, and was part of a larger conspiracy, though this has been disputed many times since then. The Committee was not able to figure out who the coconspirators were, or the identity of a second gunman, if that person existed. In 1982, the National Academy of Sciences conducted its own investigation, by studying the sounds and acoustics of the recordings of the gunfire. They decided that "reliable acoustic data do not support a conclusion that there was a second gunman." Of course, many people still disagreed with this finding and found flaws in it.

But in 2018, a new study by Dr. Nicholas Nalli examined the surviving film in detail and created models based on Kennedy's body's reactions to the shot. He was able to show that the motion of the head was consistent with being shot by the type of rifle Oswald had, and from the direction of the Texas School Book Depository, where Oswald worked. It seems that Oswald's was the killing shot.

Oswald was set up: Oswald insisted that he was set up, and some people still believe this. But if he didn't act alone, who might have been

behind it? The Soviets? Unlikely. While Oswald was sympathetic to
them, if they had authorized Kennedy's assassination, they would have
risked all-out war (probably nuclear) with the U.S. So if it wasn't a foreign enemy, who was it?

JOHN F. KENNEDY'S ASSASSINATION: THE CIA AND THE GOVERNMENT

IN DISCUSSIONS ABOUT KENNEDY'S ASSASSINATION, fingers
often point at two possible culprits: the Central Intelligence Agency
(CIA), and the United States government, possibly even including Vice
President Lyndon Johnson. What is the likelihood that either of them
could have wanted Kennedy dead?

The CIA: President Kennedy and the CIA definitely had a strained
relationship at times. The CIA was actively trying to assassinate Cuba's
leader, Fidel Castro, and Kennedy was not happy with this, as much as
anything because of the near disaster of the Cuban Missile Crisis, which
had happened a year earlier. People who believe this theory think that

Kennedy was considering shutting down the CIA altogether, and maybe even starting investigations into its activities. And those in power there didn't like that one bit.

Indeed, Allen Dulles was the former director of the CIA, and just happened to be a part of the 1964 Warren Commission, which concluded that Oswald acted alone. For some conspiracy theorists, this is a little too convenient. Was Dulles on the Committee to make sure that it reached the "right" conclusion, and didn't implicate the CIA or any of its officers?

We know that Oswald visited the Russian Embassy in Mexico a few weeks before shooting Kennedy, but no investigators have ever been able to find out what he said to them, or they to him. Again, it's doubtful that they ordered him to assassinate Kennedy, but some speculate that Oswald was working as a double agent for the CIA and the Soviets. Unless those conversations can be found on recording or in print, we'll never know.

The US government: There was some speculation that Vice President Lyndon Johnson was fed up with Kennedy and wanted him out of the way. Johnson was never seriously investigated, but some theorists maintain that he could have been involved with a plot to kill his boss. A woman named Madeleine Brown said that she had an affair with Johnson (who, like Kennedy, was known for his affairs). She claimed that she had attended a party with him, FBI Director J. Edgar Hoover, Richard Nixon, and other bigwigs the night before the assassination. She said that Johnson privately told her, "After tomorrow, those Kennedys will never embarrass me again. That's no threat. That's a promise."

If true, this would be a bombshell, a smoking gun, and every other kind of weapon you can think of! But Brown has no credibility at all. Her story seems to have been completely made up; investigators have found evidence that Johnson was never at the party as Brown claimed. She apparently lied about a lot of things. Some researchers think this rumor started because Johnson himself had many enemies, and some wanted him to look bad when he took over the presidency. Johnson had numerous flaws, but being part of a conspiracy to assassinate the president probably wasn't one of them.

JOHN F. KENNEDY'S ASSASSINATION: A MOB HIT

THE KENNEDYS ALMOST CERTAINLY HAD associations with various figures in the world of organized crime; the Mafia seemed to be everywhere in those days. There were already whispers that somehow the Mafia had helped Kennedy win the very close 1960 presidential election by tampering with votes in Illinois and in other states; accusations of voter fraud and secret fixes in elections have been going on for a long time!

But others began to suspect that Kennedy might have angered the Mafia at some other time, and one theory was that it had to do with Fidel Castro in Cuba. With Castro in control, the Florida Mafia in Miami had no way to operate its casinos in Havana and elsewhere in Cuba, as they had prior to Castro coming to power in 1959. They wanted Castro gone so the money, crime, and good times could flow again. But Kennedy wasn't able to deliver on a promise that he'd secretly made to them while running for president. Indeed, the Bay of Pigs invasion in April 1961, an attempt to overthrow Castro, ended in disaster for Cuban exiles and their US backers, and only helped Castro consolidate his power.

To make matters worse, Kennedy's brother, Robert Kennedy, was starting to crack down on organized crime in his role as US Attorney General, going after Teamsters leader Jimmy Hoffa, among others (more about him later in this chapter). This didn't sit well with those who felt they'd helped Kennedy into his job, so they decided to do something about it.

Apparently, Robert Kennedy felt that his actions did cause some kind of blowback, and he feared that his brother's death was the result of the failure to retake Cuba, and of Robert's own actions against organized crime. Robert had at first thought that the Mob might come after him, but was said to be stunned when it was John who died instead. If the Mob was sending the Kennedys a message, it was the most shocking one imaginable.

None of this is verified, of course, and may be nothing more than hearsay. Some investigators feel that there is nothing to these stories at all, as the assassination has been credited to different Mafia factions in Chicago, Miami, and even New Orleans, but without any conclusive proof. It makes for an interesting crime story, but most researchers now think that the Mob had nothing to do with it, and certainly didn't put out a hit on the president.

LEE HARVEY OSWALD'S ASSASSINATION

ON NOVEMBER 24, 1963, just two days after John F. Kennedy's assassination, his accused killer, Lee Harvey Oswald, was shot in the abdomen while being transferred from a police station to a county jail. Oswald had shaken the world with his alleged assassination of a popular president, but now he would never stand trial. He died from his gunshot wound, taking whatever he knew about those events to the grave. His killer was an unlikely man named Jack Ruby.

Ruby (real name Jacob Rubenstein) was a Dallas nightclub owner who had a history of involvement in organized crime, dating back to the 1950s. He seemed an improbable figure to go out for revenge against the man accused of killing Kennedy, and for some, this almost immediately set off alarm bells. Was this man with a tendency toward violence (he acted as his own club's bouncer!) really some super patriot who was so upset over Kennedy's death that he felt he had to kill Oswald, the accused murderer, before he could even be brought to trial? It seemed fishy, to say the least.

The most obvious explanation is that Ruby was sent by someone to silence Oswald before he had a chance to "sing" to the police or the courts. If that was the case, it meant that Oswald was not acting alone and there was—you guessed it—a conspiracy to kill the president. In fact, some would argue that much of the whole business of conspiracy theories about Kennedy's assassination comes from Ruby's actions. It seemed that in killing Oswald, someone had a lot to hide, and Oswald certainly couldn't have acted alone.

Still, the Warren Commission concluded in September 1964 that Oswald and Ruby didn't know each other, and that Oswald acted alone. This didn't sit well with a lot of people, and it still doesn't. The timing was very suspicious, and the manner of killing Oswald (a gunshot to the abdomen) was violent and swift, in keeping with a Mob-style execution. Would Ruby really have sacrificed himself to take out Oswald? Ruby went on trial and was found guilty of murder and sentenced to death, though he died of complications from lung cancer in 1967.

At his trial, Ruby's lawyer tried to use a mental-illness defense, and it was true that Ruby seemed to suffer from mood swings and erratic behavior. Is it possible that he really just was obsessed and, in the moment, decided to kill Oswald out of anger? It might be, but like Oswald, he took his secrets to the grave with him, leaving the world, and especially conspiracy theorists, to puzzle over his actions decades later.

MARTIN LUTHER KING JR.'S ASSASSINATION

THE ASSASSINATION OF civil rights leader Martin Luther King Jr. was, like Kennedy's assassination, a tragedy that sent shockwaves around the world. At 6:01 p.m., on April 4, 1968, King, staying at the Lorraine Motel in Memphis, Tennessee, was out on the balcony, speaking with friends. A single shot rang out, and a bullet hit him in the face. His injuries were severe, and while he was rushed to nearby St. Joseph's Hospital, King never regained consciousness, and died at 7:05 p.m.

A man was seen fleeing from a boarding house across the street, and shortly afterward, police found a package containing binoculars and a rifle, both of which had fingerprints that matched with a man named James Earl Ray, who was arrested in London two months later. Ray confessed to the murder, and his prints were on the rifle. It seemed to be a very easy case. Except that it wasn't. By March 1969, Ray had pleaded guilty to avoid the death penalty, but then recanted his confession, and said that he had been set up. Many people, including members of King's own family, began to doubt that Ray was a lone gunman with a grudge. Talk of a conspiracy began to circulate.

Why, for example, would Ray murder King, and then just leave behind the gun and some binoculars with his fingerprints, right where they could easily be found? It all seemed too convenient. Some began to suspect a conspiracy and a cover-up. It was long known, for example, that J. Edgar Hoover's FBI had been watching and even harassing King. The organization had called him a communist, and had tried to discredit him through lurid and false accusations about his personal life. For many, it wasn't much of a stretch to think that the FBI might have had a hand in plotting his murder.

Likewise, the Memphis police were unhappy with King and were having him watched. It was later revealed that the FBI had infiltrated the Memphis police and had their own agents in its offices.

Stories of inconsistencies circulated. One man swore that he saw a hooded gunman in some nearby bushes. Loyd Jowers, owner of the bar below the boarding house, claimed that a man came from those bushes and asked him to hide a gun. But Jowers changed his story more than once, and an investigation into his claims revealed that he was not telling the truth. Ray himself insisted that he had been in contact with a mysterious man named Raoul, who had convinced him to buy the gun and to rent the room from which Ray allegedly fired his shot. Raoul then committed the murder, leaving behind the objects with Ray's fingerprints, in an effort to frame him. It was an intriguing story, but not one that investigators were able to confirm, and Raoul, if he existed, was never found.

Whatever happened, there were too many conflicting stories to be able to piece together anything like a coherent conspiracy. Various official investigations have concluded that there was evidence both for and against a conspiracy. It is worth noting that King's son, Dexter, met with Ray in prison in 1997, and after the meeting, he left convinced that Ray was not the killer.

JIMMY HOFFA'S DISAPPEARANCE

One of the more famed disappearances of the later twentieth century, Jimmy Hoffa's case has inspired countless people to speculate on what really happened. Hoffa was a powerful union spokesman and, beginning in 1957, the president of the International Brotherhood of Teamsters. He genuinely advocated for workers, seeking higher wages, better working conditions, and so on. But early on, he also got bound up with corruption and organized crime. He was known to be involved with the Mafia on several levels, and this eventually brought him down. He was sentenced to thirteen years in prison in 1967, but in 1971, President Richard Nixon commuted his sentence, on the condition that he not do any work for unions again until 1980.

Once free, it wasn't long before Hoffa was back to his old life. Over the next few years, he started positioning himself again for a rise to power, and even worked on his autobiography. His associations with the Mafia continued, and they were probably his downfall—"probably," because not everyone thinks so.

On July 30, 1975, Hoffa disappeared from a parking lot next to the Machus Red Fox restaurant in a strip mall in Detroit. His body was never found. Almost immediately, people assumed that it was a Mob hit, but the question was, who actually did it? It turned out that a lot of people wanted him dead. There have been several suspects over the years, and many different possible fates.

Richard "The Iceman" Kuklinski, a professional hit man, claimed to have killed Hoffa by stabbing him in the head and then hiding his body in the trunk of a car that was later compacted and sold off as scrap metal.

Two federal agents abducted Hoffa and took him in a small plane to fly over the Great Lakes, where they pushed him out of the plane to his death in the water. Alternatively, Hoffa was taken into protective custody and protection, to help assist in bringing down other Mafia

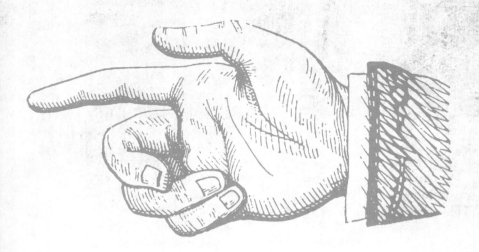

Some people believe the Mafia itself did away with Hoffa, which many consider to bethe most likely explanation. Marvin "The Weasel" Elkind, once a driver for Hoffa, claimed that the Mob killed him and dumped his body into the wet cement at the base of Detroit's Omni International Hotel when it was being built.

Another story says that Hoffa was killed and dismembered with a meat cleaver, and his body was actually hidden under the end zone of the Giants football stadium in New York!

John A. Cameron, a retired detective, claims that Hoffa was murdered by a serial killer named Edward Wayne Edwards. Edwards, he says, was responsible for any number of sensational murders from the 1940s to the 1990s. These included the Black Dahlia, JonBenét Ramsey and Laci Peterson, and he might even have been the Zodiac Killer! Yes, this seems to be stretching believability more than a little, but Cameron has done extensive research and even produced a documentary about his theories.

And, of course, the best conspiracy theory is that Hoffa faked his own death to get away from meeting a terrible fate. He escaped to Mexico and lived out his life under a new identity, away from all the troubles of the Mafia that he'd been entangled in for so long.

KOREAN AIR LINES FLIGHT 007

It was a news story that stunned the world. On September 1, 1983, Korean Air Lines Flight 007 was flying from New York to Seoul, South Korea, via Anchorage, Alaska. It should have been a routine flight, but for some reason the airplane strayed more than 200 miles into Soviet airspace (the Cold War was still raging at the time). A Soviet Su-15 interceptor jet launched missiles at the plane, striking it and bringing it down. The interceptor had first fired warning shots to get the plane to change course, but it didn't, so the pilot fired a second set of missiles. Flight 007 crashed into the Sea of Japan, killing all 269 people on board. At the time, the United States was conducting reconnaissance in the area, and the Soviets maintained that the plane was spying. If it wasn't, then it was a tragic accident, the Soviets said, one brought about by Cold War tensions and the fact that Flight 007 shouldn't have been in their airspace.

Needless to say, this "official" explanation did not sit well with many Americans, who wanted their own investigation. The whole story was fishy, and there seemed to be more to it than just an accident. President Ronald Reagan called it "an act of barbarism," and the government was quick to use the incident to ramp up anti-Soviet propaganda. The Soviets kept American and Japanese searchers away from the area, and managed to recover the plane's black box, but refused to release its contents for almost ten years, which only added to the speculation. One question everyone could agree on: Why was the plane so far off course and in forbidden airspace to begin with?

There were several theories, but the most likely was that the plane's autopilot was simply set to the wrong mode and flew off course as a result. It was an easy explanation, and when the black box recordings were finally released in 1992, this theory seemed to be proved. But other questions remained that still puzzle investigators.

How could a trained Soviet fighter pilot confuse a commercial airliner with a spy plane? He would insist that not only was it actually a spy plane, but that there were no actual passengers on board. That might seem absurd, but . . .

Where were the bodies? If the plane went down where it was claimed to have crashed, where were the bodies of the passengers and crew? Only a few body parts were ever recovered. And why was there almost no luggage in the area? Some claimed that the large Japanese spider crabs in the area probably ate the bodies (yuck!), but they wouldn't have eaten the skeletons, too! If the plane broke apart, the passengers might have been sucked out into the air and fallen to the ocean somewhere else, but again, no trace of them was found.

This has led some to speculate that the plane was damaged, but didn't crash into the ocean. Instead it made an emergency landing in the Soviet Union, and everyone on board was secretly taken prisoner and sent to Siberian and Central Asian camps. Some also claim that the United States was indeed using the plane for spying, without telling the passengers (obviously!), and after it was found out, the government had to cover up the scandal. Some even theorize that an American jet shot down the plane instead, or that there was a dogfight between Soviet and American fighter jets. The whole story is still surrounded in mystery, which means the speculation will only continue.

———————————

MALAYSIA AIRLINES FLIGHT 370

IT'S THE MOST MYSTERIOUS airline incident in modern history. On March 8, 2014, Malaysia Airlines Flight 370 departed from Kuala Lumpur International Airport, heading toward Beijing Capital International Airport. At a little over half an hour into its flight, communication with air traffic control ceased and the plane went silent. It was supposed to be in Vietnamese airspace, but made no contact with air traffic control there. Due to focusing on other matters, and perhaps mistakes or even incompetence, controllers in Malaysia didn't notice that the flight's transponder was no longer signaling. Vietnamese controllers noticed this problem, but for far too long, no one thought to contact air traffic control back in Malaysia. The Vietnamese did try repeatedly to contact Flight 370, but got no response. The plane simply disappeared from radar, and it was hours before a search was begun, right about the time the plane should have been arriving in Beijing. But, of course, it never did.

It took several days and detailed reviews of other radar systems to discover that once the plane reached Vietnamese airspace, it turned sharply southwest and flew toward the Andaman Sea (west of Thailand). After that, it simply passed out of radar detection and vanished. Of course, this story is absurd. A Boeing 777 airliner with that much technical equipment on board cannot simply "vanish," yet that's exactly what happened.

It didn't appear to be a hijacking, because nothing came of it, neither demands nor a terrorist attack. It didn't seem to be a pilot suicide, because this didn't resemble any known pilot suicide in the past. The plane just mysteriously veered off course, ended all contact, and disappeared. But it didn't escape detection completely. Various systems were able to track something over the Indian Ocean that cruised at altitude for some time before beginning a sharp descent to the water. It was not an attempt to land, but appeared to be a crash. So what happened? Did it run out of fuel? Did the pilot indeed want to commit suicide?

There were several mysteries. The plane might have had power issues, or there could have been a loss of air pressure that literally knocked out or killed everyone on board. Two passengers were found to have boarded the plane with stolen passports, but they seem to have been asylum seekers, not terrorists. Also, the aircraft was carrying a large cargo of lithium-ion batteries, which in rare circumstances can explode. And, of course, the pilot was investigated. Although a route similar to the one taken by Flight 370 was found on his flight simulator, investigators found nothing to indicate that he was suicidal. The flight did pass over Penang, the pilot's home island, and would have afforded him a long, last look at it, if that's what he wanted.

Conspiracy theorists have many ideas: hijackers or hackers took control of the plane and landed it somewhere, while making it look like it crashed; the US military shot it down after learning that it was flying on a terrorist mission; it was diverted to Pakistan for future terrorist plans; and, of course, aliens took the whole plane, or it flew into a wormhole and entered another dimension/time, or it was destroyed by a tiny black hole, and so on.

While pieces of debris have been collected in the area of the southern Indian Ocean where the flight is presumed to have crashed, the truth is still out there. That such a giant machine could so completely disappear means that conspiracy theories about its fate will be with us for a long time.

MALAYSIA AIRLINES FLIGHT 17

AS IF MALAYSIA AIRLINES didn't have enough problems with the loss of Flight 370, only four months later, an equally shocking tragedy occurred. Flight 17 was shot down over Ukraine on July 17, 2014. The flight had left Amsterdam's airport and was bound for Kuala Lumpur, Malaysia. It broke up in the air over Ukraine, and investigators were able to determine that it had been brought down by a Russian-made Buk ground-to-air missile. The devastating attack killed everyone on board.

Almost immediately, the finger-pointing and blaming began. Ukraine at the time was locked in a terrible civil war, with rebels backed by Russia on one side. So, the first thought was that Russians or the rebels shot the plane down, mistakenly thinking it was a Ukrainian air force jet. It was not their intention to murder civilians, so the theory goes.

But just as quickly, people doubted this, and alternate theories began to spring up. Russia itself denied any involvement, and accused Ukraine of deliberately rerouting the plane to fly over the war zone. They said that a Ukrainian fighter jet had shot down Flight 17. Investigations into this version of events tended to show that the damage to the plane could not have come from the missiles on a fighter jet, but only from one launched from the ground. Some Russian sources then backtracked and tried to say that yes, it had been a ground-to-air missile, but one that belonged to Ukraine, not the rebels.

And so this back-and-forth went on, with bits and pieces of evidence for all views surfacing now and then as the investigation continued. After months of research, it does seem that a rebel-held missile launcher brought down the plane, even if the rebels didn't intend to do so, despite what they and the Russians said. About the only point that both sides could agree on was that Ukraine should have been diverting passenger planes outside of the airspace of the conflict to keep them away from danger.

But, of course, the internet being what it is, it wasn't long before alternate theories started popping up, some of them from Russia itself. Sergei Sokolov, head of a Russian security organization, claimed that the CIA planted explosives on board and blew up the plane to embarrass Russia and President Putin. Others claimed that the secret organization known as the Illuminati (see the Secret Societies chapter) ordered the plane to be shot down for reasons unknown.

Another Russian, Igor Girkin, claimed that the flight was full of dead bodies when it took off from Amsterdam! The point, he said, was to stage a "tragedy" to blame Russia, but not have to kill anyone to do it. This bizarre excuse has no evidence at all, by the way. Similarly, some theorists have said that the New World Order (see the Secret Societies chapter) had the plane shot down to broaden the conflict in the area, and pull many nations into another world war.

The Russian newspaper *Pravda* reported that NATO may have thought Putin was flying in the area at the time, and ordered the plane shot down to try to assassinate him. But Putin wasn't in the area on that day. Other stories blamed various people and countries, but the official explanation really is the best one, in this case.

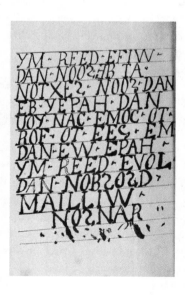

THE CLINTON "BODY COUNT"

BOTH WIDELY LOVED AND LOATHED, Bill and Hillary Clinton
have been subjected to numerous accusations and conspiracy theories
since Bill's time as president in the 1990s. One of the more prominent
accusations, picked up and run with by his political opponents, is the
idea that so-called enemies of the Clintons seem to die in high numbers and in mysterious circumstances. In other words, they have a long
history of having their opponents murdered. This idea took shape in the
early 1990s, and still pops up from time to time.

The notion first appeared in 1993, when a lawyer from Indianapolis
named Linda Thompson produced a list called "The Clinton Body
Count: Coincidence or the Kiss of Death?" This list contained thirty-four names of people she said had ties to the Clintons and had died
mysteriously. Right from the start, Thompson admitted that she had no
evidence for any of these deaths being caused or ordered by the Clintons, and said that orders to kill might have come from "people trying
to control the president," though she never said who she thought those
people were, or how they would be able to control him. Her claims were
taken up by Representative William Dannemeyer, a Clinton opponent
who cut the list down to twenty-four and claimed that all of them had
died in mysterious circumstances while having close ties to the Clintons. He wanted an official investigation.

Contrary to some claims, the mainstream media did do several investigations into these allegations, and found nothing unusual. There are a
number of websites that look at each dead individual in detail, showing how their deaths were not nearly as "mysterious" as some like to
claim. A lot of word twisting and ignoring of facts go on with such lists
(dealing with the Clintons and others). And these lists almost always
ignore the fact that there are often people who are alive and kicking,
even though they have much more damaging information about the
person in question. The dead are often people who have the thinnest of
connections to the accused, and who were not in much of a position to
do anything anyway: "Clinton's barber's brother was in a 'car accident.'
But that's just what they want you to believe. . . ."

One of the big problems with lists like these is that new names were (and still are) added, while old ones were taken off, so that now there are several versions of the list, especially circulating among modern QAnon believers (see the Politics chapter). So, which list is official? Are those that were removed no longer victims?

The Clintons were hardly scandal free, but hit lists like these do a disservice to any real investigations into public figures that might be warranted. These lists and conspiracies usually come from political hatred and a desire to see "the enemy" crushed, not from any real evidence of wrongdoing or criminal behavior.

CHAPTER 3
SECRET SOCIETIES

THE IDEA OF SINISTER, secret societies pulling the strings behind the scenes is almost irresistible. It helps many people explain why so much seems to go wrong in the world every day, and why nothing ever seems to improve, not really, anyway. It's as if a shadowy cabal wants things to keep getting worse so that it can tighten its grip on power and rule the world, while most of us remain ignorant about what's really going on. And there's a strange kind of comfort in this belief: if we're all puppets on strings, then we're not really responsible for the bad things around us, and we can't do much to make good things happen anyway.

We all feel powerless from time to time; it's especially frustrating if those who have power seem to get away with actions and even crimes that we never could. It's as if they're receiving help from some source, a wealthy elite that can bail them out and prop them up. But do secretive organizations really run the world, or at least sow chaos and destruction for their own reasons? Here is a collection of several examples of such societies that might make you wonder.

THE SATANIC PANIC OF THE 1980S

ONE OF THE MORE DRAMATIC PIECES of panic and mass hysteria in the 1980s was a series of rumors that grew into a widespread belief that secret cults of Satanists were kidnapping children, and then raping and murdering them in their rituals. Originating in some religious fundamentalist circles, the idea of "satanic cults among us" played on age-old fears about mysterious people and "others" in the midst of "respectable" society. We've already seen how this went in Salem, Massachusetts, in the 1690s, and the attitude wasn't all that far off from that in the 1980s. But this time, the witch hunt also involved politicians, therapists, social workers, and others who thought they were doing genuine good. The idea of satanic ritual abuse took hold, and even when there was no evidence, belief in it was enough to keep the whole thing going.

The idea was not without some truth. The 1960s and 1970s had included Charles Manson's circle, serial killers, an increased interest in occult topics, and other dark phenomena. It was enough to make people nervous. The rise of evangelicals and self-proclaimed "experts" on the occult came about by the 1980s; the culture was ripe for paranoia and false accusations.

In 1980, a memoir called *Michelle Remembers* was published and became a best seller. In it, author and psychologist Lawrence Pazder claimed to have helped a patient uncover shocking repressed memories of childhood satanic abuse at the hands of a secret cult. The book was easily disproven by some serious investigations, but not before it became a kind of handbook for those trying to root out secret cults. The parallels between Salem's paranoia and the fifteenth-century *Malleus Maleficarum* (a handbook for uncovering witches) were easily apparent, but by then too many people were swept up in their own fear; history was repeating itself.

Social workers and police began believing that day care centers were hotbeds of satanic cult activity, and that the children in their care were being taken away and abused in dark rituals, and then warned to stay silent about it. Unlicensed therapists were given access to children and started coercing confessions from them, often getting the

answers they wanted to hear. Accusations starting flying, and often people were arrested and went to trial. Some of these trials fell apart due to lack of evidence, but in too many cases, people went to prison for years, even decades, before their convictions were overturned. The morbid fantasies of conspiracy theorists did real harm to a lot of innocent people.

The craze died down in the early 1990s, and the United States Department of Justice released a guide for investigators on how to approach these cases. It stated that there was no sign of any systematic ritual abuse going on in the United States, and provided the evidence to back up its claims.

Of course, there is also a larger conspiracy theory that suggests the entire "satanic panic" was invented by certain guilty politicians to dodge investigations into their own pedophile rings and activities. By diverting people's fears toward the idea of deadly secret cults, they could better hide what they were doing. There will always be another theory larger than the last one.

THE ILLUMINATI

AH, THE ILLUMINATI! You can't have a book about conspiracy theories without talking about them. They're probably the most famous of all secret societies, even if most people have no idea who they are supposed to be and what they're accused of doing. They're a go-to for almost every conspiracy theory that has ever existed. Somehow, this group of secretive elites is behind nearly all the bad things that happen in the world: wars, political instability, assassinations, turmoil, all to keep their grip on power. But who are these mysterious people, and what do they really do? Is there an actual Illuminati out there somewhere, pulling the strings? Or is it all just a figment of overactive imaginations?

Well, there really was an Illuminati, based in Bavaria and founded in 1776 by the German philosopher Johann Adam Weishaupt. The group was intended to embrace Enlightenment ideals and reject superstition and religious control of public affairs. This made them immediately unpopular with the Catholic Church and the authorities in Bavaria, and they, along with other secret societies, were outlawed. But they continued to operate in secret, of course, and some people (then and now) believed that they were partly responsible for the French Revolution. In fact, the group only lasted about ten years, and had, at most, no more than 2,500 members . . . or at least that's what they want you to believe!

The Illuminati endeavored to control politics—and, yes, even the world—through secretive influences. They sought to bring reason to politics, and wanted to use their philosophies to influence those in office and infiltrate the corridors of power. Sounds like a sinister secret group, right? In reality, their goals were relatively noble, it seems, and they didn't have much influence at all. Secret societies were banned by Karl Theodor, Duke in Bavaria, in 1785, and the Illuminati sort of fizzled out. Or . . . did they?

Conspiracy theories about the group have been around ever since, and believers will tell you that the group went underground and only increased in power. The founders of the United States, many of whom were Freemasons (more on them later), portrayed the Illuminati as a threat (the Illuminati had tried to recruit new members by going to Freemason lodges and infiltrating them), and at one point, Thomas Jefferson was accused of being a member.

The group faded from public awareness over time, though there were probably some who still feared its influence. The concept of a secret Illuminati society was given new life in the mid-1970s, with the publication of *The Illuminatus! Trilogy* by authors Robert Shea and Robert Anton Wilson, who weaved a bizarre, psychedelic, post-counterculture story into their books and gave popularity once again to the concept of secret societies manipulating things behind the scenes, a perfectly good explanation for everything bad that had happened since Kennedy's assassination. From there, many conspiracy theorists jumped on the idea that the Illuminati had never really gone away, but had indeed been influencing world events ever since the eighteenth century. It was very easy to slot them into anything that seemed suspicious.

And so, the Illuminati are with us again. Watching, always watching . . .

———————————

THE SKULL AND BONES SOCIETY
AT YALE UNIVERSITY

WHILE PEOPLE DEBATE about the existence of the Illuminati and other such groups, it's a fact that there are actually many existing secretive societies around the world. These organizations often limit their memberships to an exclusive few, usually the very wealthy and privileged. It's only natural that these groups would be the targets of suspicion and resentment among those who are not invited into their inner sanctums. One such group is the Skull and Bones Society at Yale University.

Also known as The Order (a rather sinister-sounding name!) and Order 322, Skull and Bones was founded in 1832 for Yale University seniors. The society continues to operate, and continues to be exclusive; each year, only fifteen Yale seniors are tapped for membership. These members have included three presidents—William Howard Taft (whose father cofounded the society), George H. W. Bush, and George W. Bush—as well as countless others who have taken prominent places in society. While the names of its members are often public, these folks tend to be very secretive about the society itself, even years later. In the 2004 presidential election, both candidates—George W. Bush and John Kerry—had been members. When asked about their time in the society, Bush said that the group's activities were so secret that he couldn't talk about them, while Kerry half-joked, "Are you trying to get rid of me here?" Kerry also dismissed the idea that two "Bonesmen" running against each other meant much of anything. Of course, if they already rule everything in secret, he would say that!

Such talk has only fueled speculation that the society hides some truly sinister secrets. The usual suspicion is that the group is a recruiting organization for college students from very wealthy families into an older organization that secretly controls the world, or wants to. Some believe that the Skull and Bones Society is a branch of the Illuminati, while others think that it actually controls the CIA and directs all of the horrible things that the CIA is accused of doing. Indeed, one member, James Jesus Angleton, headed CIA counterintelligence for almost twenty years, which, for believers, is about as much proof as they need—the proverbial smoking gun. As you might have guessed, some blame Skull and Bones for the Kennedy assassination, among other crimes.

The group meets in a building on campus called the "Tomb," and only society members are allowed to enter. The Tomb is rumored to house the skulls of President Martin van Buren, Mexican revolutionary Pancho Villa, and even the Apache warrior Geronimo. Geronimo's skull is said to have been stolen and brought to the Tomb by Prescott Bush, President George H. W. Bush's father. But the truth is that these stories are nothing more than rumors and have never been proven.

The number "322" is also associated with the society, and seems to refer to the year 322 BCE, when the Greek orator Demosthenes died. At that time, Athens transitioned from a democracy to a plutocracy (government by the elite and wealthy), and some see this as proof that the society wants to abolish democracy in the United States and replace it with a plutocracy of its own members.

What really goes on inside those mysterious Skull and Bones gatherings? We don't know, but it seems to be a case of members saying, "I could tell you, but I'd have to kill you."

THE FREEMASONS

THE FREEMASONS ARE A BONA FIDE, actual, existing group.
They've been around for centuries. They have secret initiations and
rituals. They've had some very famous members over the years: Mozart,
George Washington, Thomas Jefferson, Franklin D. Roosevelt, Winston
Churchill, Duke Ellington, Nat King Cole, and even John Wayne. Some
claim that they are the modern descendants of the medieval Knights
Templar, a monastic military order that was suppressed in the early
fourteenth century because its members were too powerful and knew
too much.

Indeed, as recently as the 1980s, the Freemasons have been condemned
by the Catholic Church, which forbids Catholics from being members
(though how well they can enforce this is anyone's guess). The Ortho-
dox Church says something similar. The Masons have been portrayed
as both a harmless cultural and charitable organization and a sinister,
cultlike group with hidden influence, which, like the Illuminati, pulls
the strings on world events, manipulating them in favor of the elite,
rich, and powerful.

But who are they, really? Well, they might not be modern Templars, but
the idea of the group could go back to the Middle Ages, when stonema-
sons who worked on the cathedrals formed guilds to train others and

protect their interests. Documents about a Mason-like group date from the early fifteenth century, and Masonic historians like to point to these as proof of how old their group is. But these mentions were probably more for trade organizations than the modern version of the group. What is known is that some form of Masonic secret society existed by the later seventeenth century (though the Edinburgh Lodge claims to have been up and running since 1598), and it drew thinkers of all kinds. The group became quite popular in the eighteenth century, attracting some very famous people to its membership.

The Masons have secret rituals and meetings, and even secret hand-shakes. They meet in local chapters called Lodges, which are closed to outsiders. They have degrees and ranks that new members have to work their way up to over time. They insist it's all benign, a way for people with common interests to meet, socialize, and exchange ideas. But some don't believe that. The Masons have been accused of everything from Satanism and political interference to controlling NASA in order to hide evidence of alien life from the world (seriously). Anti-Semitic groups have sometimes accused the Freemasons of being in league with the Jews (or even being controlled by them) in a quest for world domina-tion. In fact, Freemasons were persecuted by the Nazis, and it's thought that well over 100,000 of them may have died. It is true (as with any old, exclusive club) that the Masons have been problematic in dealing with women and those who are nonwhite, to say the least.

In any case—so say conspiracy theorists—when new members join the organization, they are not told about any of the secret knowledge of the society, even if they are curious about it. Only over time, and after they have proven their loyalty and worked their way up through the ranks, will the true secrets of Masonry be revealed. The Masonic agenda is as insidious as that of their enemies, the Illuminati, say some believers. Who knows what kind of behind-the-scenes battles for control of the world are raging without us even knowing it?

THE ROSICRUCIANS

THE ROSICRUCIANS HAVE A FANCY NAME (it means "rosy cross")
and a pretty fancy history, too, dating back to the seventeenth century.
The so-called "Order of the Rosy Cross" announced itself to Europe
in 1614 with three works that told of the order's until-then unknown
history. According to these documents, a German nobleman named
Christian Rosenkreuz was born in 1378 and lived for 106 years. During
his life, he traveled widely and studied not only Christian mysticisms
but Sufism and possibly Zoroastrianism, among other traditions. He
eventually tried to spread his knowledge to educated people, but they
mostly rejected him, so he gathered together a small group of eight, who
vowed to study and live by the principles he had learned, but in secret.
As each one grew old and neared death, a replacement would be chosen,
so that there would always be eight members.

In the seventeenth century, the group finally announced itself to the world, stating that it was seeking to expand and to transform scientific knowledge with knowledge of true alchemy and philosophy. This news was exciting to some, while others saw the whole thing as a big hoax. If you were a genuine member of the Rosicrucians, you were not supposed to admit to it, so it made tracking the group down rather difficult, to say the least. Still, there were many young thinkers, philosophers, scientists, and dreamers who were very willing to sign up and join. But the Rosicrucians, if they existed, still didn't show their faces. Presumably, if one were worthy, one would simply "know" how to find the order and join in secret, without announcing it to anyone.

That might have been the end of the matter, but by the close of the seventeenth century, other versions of the Rosicrucians started popping up, some of whom were intertwined with the Freemasons, giving the whole thing an even more mysterious air. Were these simply wannabe groups, trying to capitalize off the name? Probably, but some of them claimed to be the "true" order, so who knows? The Rosicrucians claimed to work for the betterment of society (like most secretive organizations), and as hidden orders go, they have been seen as more benign than some of the groups accused of scheming behind the scenes. There are several modern groups that use the name, some claiming that their knowledge goes back to ancient Egypt. These are mostly charitable and philanthropic entities, with no obvious desires to rule the world (that we know of . . .).

The Rosicrucians represented more of a philosophy than an actual group. Different organizations took on aspects of that philosophy and adapted them to their individual needs, such as the Masons. It's likely that Rosenkreuz and his story are completely fictional, but it gave this blend of magic, philosophy, alchemy, and science a way of grounding itself in the real world, and of having more influence on other groups than even its inventors probably would have thought possible.

THE PRIORY OF SION

A SMALL GROUP OF PEOPLE IN EUROPE is rumored by some to hold the most dangerous secrets of all, at least as far as Western civilization is concerned. The Priory of Sion, according to certain conspiracy theorists, is a very old organization, founded in the year 1099 by a French knight, Godfrey of Bouillon. He created it after the end of the First Crusade, when Christian Europe retook Jerusalem from the Muslims who held it at the time. The Priory created the Knights Templar, based on its discoveries while excavating under Jerusalem, and it developed certain goals, one of which was the restoration of the Merovingian royal line to the French throne.

Why would they care about this? Well, that's the big shocker. The Priory was said to have proof that Jesus did not die on the cross, but rather came to France with Mary Magdalene, who was his wife, and their children. Since Jesus himself was descended from the line of King David, these children were members of an ancient royal bloodline, one that eventually established itself as the ruling monarchs of France from the sixth through the eighth centuries. The Priory was secretly devoted to returning this bloodline to power, not only in France, but across Europe.

The Catholic Church has tried to suppress and destroy the Priory, because the Priory knows the truth, so the theory goes. A popular legend speaks of a parish priest who, in the southern French village of Rennes-le-Château, discovered something in the church that made him a rich man. What he found wasn't material wealth, but information proving Jesus's survival and bloodline decent, which he was able to use to blackmail the Church into buying his silence.

Allegedly, the Priory has been headed by many famous names throughout history, including Leonardo da Vinci, Isaac Newton, Victor Hugo, and Claude Debussy, and in the mid- to later twentieth century, by a mysterious man named Pierre Plantard. Plantard claimed to be the latest in a long series of these Grand Masters, taking over in 1956, but some deeper investigating revealed that all was not as it seemed. Plantard had been convicted of fraud in 1953, and the "Priory of Sion" seems to have been invented by him and a few friends in 1956 as an antigovernment

group. But Plantard's imagination took over, and he fabricated a whole fantastical history and planted "clues" around the country to back it up. So-called "secret documents" that supported his claims were later found to have been forged.

In the early 1980s, authors Henry Lincoln, Michael Baigent, and Richard Leigh wrote a controversial best seller, *The Holy Blood and the Holy Grail*, which discussed the whole matter and concluded that it was genuine. While most now dismiss *The Holy Blood* as nothing more than fiction based on fraud, it spawned a whole industry of other speculative books and investigations, each seeming to come up with more fantastic conclusions than the one before it. Dan Brown's popular novel, *The Da Vinci Code*, took the story even further.

But Plantard even admitted in the 1990s that he made the whole thing up. This confession was part of a plea agreement after police raided his home in 1993 and found evidence of hoaxing. So the Priory seems to be nothing more than a modern hoax, but one that had a very good run in conspiracy circles for several decades.

THE BILDERBERG GROUP

THE ANNUAL BILDERBERG MEETING, so-called because the first meeting in 1954 took place at the Bilderberg Hotel in the Netherlands, is a gathering of political figures, business leaders, financial representatives, members of academia, and others. Its original stated purpose was to bring thinkers together to figure out how to prevent another world war, but more recently, it is focused on strengthening ties between Europe and the United States, promoting free markets, and any other issues it sees fit to discuss. Attendance is limited to an exclusive number, usually no more than 150. The group releases a list of the topics that will be discussed at the meeting, and who will attend, but those attendees are not allowed to go into detail about who said what. In theory, this is to allow free discussion of any subject without a fear of backlash, but as you can imagine, it has also given conspiracy theorists of all types plenty of ammo to think about what's really going on at those meetings! After all, if what they're talking about is completely innocent, why are they keeping so much of it hidden? Why are so few people invited?

So what does the group want, and what are they trying to do? That depends on who you ask. Those on the right think the Bilderberg Group

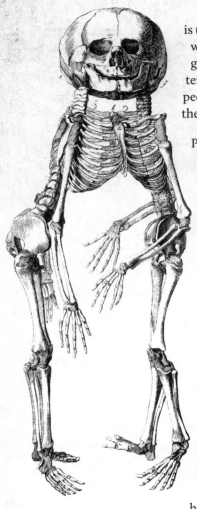

is (still) trying to impose world communism, while those on the left often think that the group is trying to promote further unfettered capitalism, regardless of the costs to people and the world, so long as they make themselves rich in the process.

People who have attended these meetings have admitted that they do discuss policies that are sometimes later taken up by governments, but they say that's not being secretive, it's just the way things are done. Anonymous attendees have talked about the experience, and they insist that while the meetings are private, that is to protect everyone involved, not to impose some hidden agenda on the world. In fact, some have insisted that they are very much against dictatorships, terrorism, and other world problems, and that these topics are regularly discussed.

That explanation is not good enough for many, of course, who insist that the whole group is a vast conspiracy, basically hiding in plain sight. Famous world leaders, such as Margaret Thatcher, Bill Clinton, and Tony Blair, have all been to these meetings, which only "proves" that the Bilderberg Group controls them all. Of course, there are those who take it much further and link the group to the anti-Semitic conspiracies, wherein the Jews want to rule the world.

Putting aside such offensive nonsense, some other critics do have a point. Realistically, a gathering of elites in politics and business is going to do very little to change the world, since all they're doing is talking to each other, not to the people directly affected by big policies. It's very easy to pat each other on the back in these kinds of meetings, rather than committing to fixing actual problems, and that might be the real issue with a secretive society like the Bilderberg Group.

THE NEW WORLD ORDER

THE "NEW WORLD ORDER" is something of an umbrella term among certain groups of conspiracy theorists (often right wing or Christian fundamentalist) that refers to a secret cabal of wealthy elites who desire to control the world. They have a globalist agenda to install a one-world, communist-style government that will take away freedoms from everyone. The group has already succeeded in capturing much of the world, the theory goes, but some believe that the United States is one of the last nations to hold out, though it is at risk of falling soon, too. It ties into paranoid fears about the loss of liberty through excessive government regulations, as well as beliefs among some Christian groups that the end of the world is near. In other words, it can mean different things to different people, but the overall idea is pretty much the same.

The New World Order, according to these believers, controls everything behind the scenes: economies, governments, wars, terrorist attacks, pandemics, you name it! All of it is designed to make the public weaker, more depressed, and open to accepting more restrictions on their freedoms so that when the final takeover happens, they will be too beaten down to resist it. And that time is getting closer. Many conspiracy theorists who believe in this reality also think that there have been dozens, if not hundreds, of secret concentration camps built in the United States, waiting to hold anyone who resists. The New World Order intends to spy on everyone, cull the population, and implement mind control to turn everyone into slaves.

So who is behind the evil plans of the New World Order? You name it: the Illuminati, the Freemasons, the Jews, the communists, the socialists, the Nazis who fled Germany after World War II, the reptilian aliens (see the UFOs & Other Unknowns chapter), some other aliens, the Democrats, antigun groups, the gays, the Satanists, the Muslims . . .

As you can see, there is no shortage of people to blame and focus hate on. And that is one of the biggest weaknesses of any theory like this. It can literally be adapted to fit any scenario and any group that someone wants to hate and blame. As such, it's not a coherent theory at all, just a mess of paranoid ramblings that tries to connect dots between things that can't be connected. If someone wants to believe in something badly enough, they'll find the evidence they need to back it up, even if that evidence is nonsense. There are endless internet discussion groups where believers post their "proofs" and whip each other into a frenzy about the imminent takeover. They've been doing it for years and show no signs of stopping now.

THE NORTH AMERICAN UNION

THE NORTH AMERICAN UNION doesn't exist, at least not in any real way. In theory, it would be something like the European Union: an alliance of different nations with a single currency, allowing for freedom of movement and employment between Canada, the United States, and Mexico. It's an economic idea that has been floated for a long time, and which has taken on a life of its own among conspiracy theorists of all political persuasions. The left sees it as a way for corporations to gain more power and sidestep environmental and labor regulations, while the right fears a loss of US sovereignty and currency, and foreign courts telling the United States what it can and cannot do. The ultimate plan would be to dissolve the United States altogether and merge the three nations into one.

Conspiracy theorists who worry about this plan bring up the Security and Prosperity Partnership of North America (SPP), which is really just made up of groups in the three countries who get together to discuss various issues of concern to all three nations: energy, transportation, the environment, immigration, and so on. But SPP is something much more sinister, some claim. It's a secret group plotting to force integration between the three nations (potentially moving millions of people from one country to another), and to persecute people of certain beliefs for having those beliefs.

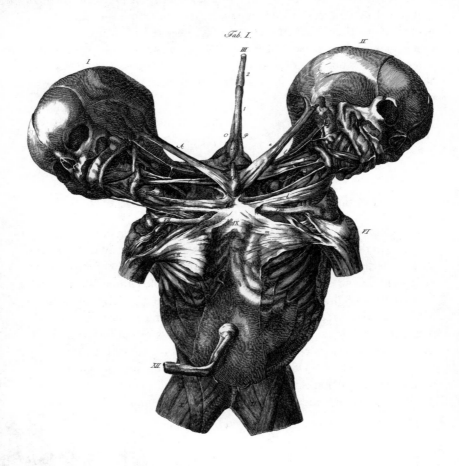

These fears are rampant among conspiracy theorists who lean far to the right and to religious fundamentalism. They are truly terrified by the idea of an international Big Brother coming along to take away their rights to believe what they want. There's even a fear that the CANAMEX corridor, a series of highways linking Mexico to Canada across the Western United States, will be used for nefarious purposes. Some say that Mexico will be able to claim certain US territories as their own. There is also a fear that the US dollar will be replaced by a currency called the "amero," which would be used in all three countries. The United States would then be subject to the whims of foreign governments.

Of course, all of this sounds very much like the concerns about the European Union, and those who oppose the supposed North American Union usually oppose the EU for similar reasons. And there is no small amount of racism lying behind several of these fears, espousing "keep Mexicans in Mexico" while never voicing the same concerns about Canadians trying to claim US territory or settle in the United States.

It's just one more fear to keep people whipped into a frenzy, without any real evidence to back it up. There are no plans for an NAU, and it's something that no politician of any political persuasion would propose, because it would damage their popularity.

CHAPTER 4
POLITICS

PROBABLY THE MOST DIVISIVE TOPIC TODAY, political arguments have seemed to get more intense and worse in recent years. Of course, this opens the door for all sorts of conspiracy theories about how the other side is working in secret to destroy the nation, the world, etc. Two of the conspiracies in this chapter actually happened: MK-Ultra and Operation Northwoods. Both were massive failures in government regulation and oversight which showed that sometimes a department within government can go too far and cause terrible harm. Other events, such as the Oklahoma City bombing, leave investigators with genuine questions, and many level-headed researchers think that more happened than we've been told.

Some of the other conspiracy theories in this chapter are nothing more than the product of overactive imaginations and partisan hatred, but they have also caused some real harm. Politics and conspiracy theories are very often not a good combination, no matter how much one wants to believe in them.

MK-ULTRA

THERE ARE A LOT OF CONSPIRACY THEORIES out there about secret government operations and programs, things done in the shadows that advanced some evil agenda and caused terrible harm. While the majority of these turn out to be nonsense, no more than fantastical paranoia, every once in a while, along comes a disturbing story about a secret government operation that happens to be true. This is the case with the infamous MK-Ultra, a project of the CIA. It was an appalling attempt by the government to study things it had no business studying, while inflicting real harm on the test subjects.

In early April 1953, the US government and intelligence agencies were becoming increasingly alarmed by the thought that the Soviets were successfully capturing and brainwashing subjects and instilling communist ideologies in them. They worried that POWs from the Korean War who were being returned might have been changed into unwitting Soviet spies, whether by hypnosis, drugs, or some other method. The director of the CIA, Allen Dulles, used the term "brain warfare" and saw this as a new frontier in the growing Cold War between the United States and the USSR. He and others were determined that the United States had to get in on it to keep up. In short, they had to learn about mind control and how to do it!

But how does an agency do that? How do you figure out how to control people's thoughts and make them do what you want? You have to do it without telling them, of course! Some of the people the MK-Ultra program brought in for experimentation were volunteers. They were criminals who were serving time, and they were offered reduced sentences and other perks if they volunteered. But they often didn't know what was going to happen to them. Several were given doses of LSD to see what kinds of reactions they would have, but they were never told what was going on.

Famed crime boss Whitey Bulger took part in an LSD experiment and wrote about it: "The room would change shape. Hours of paranoia and feeling violent. We experienced horrible periods of living nightmares and even blood coming out of the walls. Guys turning to skeletons in

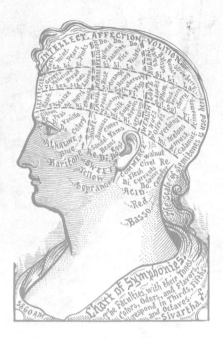

front of me. I saw a camera change into the head of a dog. I felt like I was going insane."

It wasn't just inmates who were experimented on. The mentally ill, soldiers, those deemed to be socially "deviant," and a host of other test subjects were given drugs, hypnotized, and treated with shocks and electrocution, all in an attempt to see what might make them submissive enough to be controlled.

As you might imagine, this was a civil rights nightmare and an absolutely outrageous breach of American laws. The CIA had to keep it secret, because if the truth got out, it would be devastating. The program was quietly shut down in 1963, but in 1977, a committee was formed to investigate its practices. Unfortunately, by then a lot of the documents had been destroyed. Still, many conspiracy theorists believe that MK-Ultra, or a version of it, is still running in secret, still working on perfecting the art of mind control.

FLUORIDATION
OF DRINKING WATER

FLUORIDE IS A NATURALLY OCCURRING mineral that is released from rocks, and it can be found in soil and water in trace amounts. It is known to have many beneficial properties for the health of teeth. It's a common ingredient in toothpaste, and in various places in the United States and elsewhere, small amounts of it are added to drinking water. The idea is that it will help children's teeth grow stronger and be better protected against cavities, especially children in poorer areas. But not everyone accepts this dental-health explanation. Fluoride in water, they say, has much more evil possibilities and consequences.

The idea that there is something sinister about fluoride in our drinking water is nothing new. In the 1950s and 1960s, many people believed that fluoride was a mind-control drug that was being added to water so that American kids could be lured into embracing communism (along with everything else suspect, apparently), or at least to make them weak so they couldn't defend themselves when those commie tanks came rolling up.

More recently, many have expressed a genuine concern that fluoride might not be that good for our overall health, and that its effects on dental health are not great enough to justify putting it in a water supply. Those with bigger fears claim that fluoride lowers a person's IQ over time, and can lead to a number of health problems, including dementia and Alzheimer's disease in later life.

While the "Red Scare" conspiracy theory about fluoride went away after the 1960s, there are those on the fringes of the health and New Age movements who continue to see fluoride as doing many of the same things that the anticommunists feared back at the height of the Cold War. Various websites and publications claim that low doses of fluoride over time erode a person's ability to resist orders and commands. The real point of fluoride, they say, is to make the population docile and receptive to whatever the government tells them, without even knowing that it's happening to them, a claim backed up by the assertion that the Germans and Soviets added the mineral to the drinking water at prison camps.

In any case, there is growing concern about the effects of fluoride, and a fear among some people that the government might be hiding test results that it doesn't want the public to hear, if for no other reason than it would be an embarrassing backtrack to have to make after decades of saying that fluoride in water is safe. As a result, more than seventy cities around the United States have now removed fluoride from their drinking water, a sign that the concern is a real one, conspiracy theories or not.

A ROMAN CATHOLIC TAKEOVER OF THE UNITED STATES

CONSPIRACY THEORIES ABOUT the Roman Catholic Church go back a long way in the history of the United States. In a nation made up of largely Protestant believers in its early decades, it was perhaps only natural that conspiracies about Catholic attempts to undermine the new country would spring up. Of course, this wasn't helped by early territorial disputes with Mexico, a very Catholic country. There had been a long tradition in European Protestant belief of pointing out how the Catholic Church was actually the diabolical in disguise, and that sentiment transferred over pretty easily to beliefs in the United States.

Throughout the nineteenth century, a good number of books were published to alert "real Americans" and "real Christians" to the nefarious activities of the Roman Catholic Church. Conspiracy theories about all sorts of plots sprang up, most of which said that the pope in Rome was behind them, and that the point was to undermine the United States and turn it into a nation that would be subjugated to Rome and the Catholic Church.

These fears gave rise to increasing anti-immigrant sentiment against people arriving in America from Catholic countries, especially Ireland and Italy, and allowed for full-scale discrimination against them. These people were almost always segregated and forced to live in their own communities. They were frequently denied the chance for jobs, and usually were not made to feel welcome at all.

In the 1850s, a political party called the Know Nothings based its platform on a nativist agenda, and insisted that all of these immigrants were coming to the United States for the purpose of overthrowing it, with the pope's blessing. Catholic bishops were organizing potential voters to get themselves elected to positions of importance, and then the real work would begin. It was the duty of American Protestants, the Know Nothings insisted, to stand up and resist this insidious secret plot. As a political party, they didn't last very long, but their attitudes remained strong among many for a long time afterward.

This paranoia waxed and waned over the decades, but it had something of a revival during the 1960 presidential election race between John F. Kennedy and Richard Nixon. Kennedy was Catholic, and for some, this rang alarm bells. They warned that Protestant blood would run in the streets if Kennedy was elected, and that this was what the Church had been secretly working for over a long period of time: a U.S. president who would bow to Rome and do what it wanted. Of course, Kennedy won the election and nothing much happened at all, at least in terms of the pope assuming the leadership of the United States. But fears of a Catholic conspiracy persisted for some, and became a featured belief of some evangelical groups over the next few decades.

OPERATION NORTHWOODS

AMONG THE MANY, MANY CONSPIRACY THEORIES out there, some have a grain of truth to them. And some turn out to be completely true. Such is the case with Operation Northwoods, a plan at the height of the Cold War to provoke a military conflict with Cuba. Alarmed by a Soviet-supported, communist nation virtually in its backyard, US government officials were keen to depose or assassinate Fidel Castro (who had come to power in 1959), and had investigated ways to bring this about. After the disastrous failure of the Bay of Pigs invasion in 1961, the Department of Defense started floating new ideas to bring down Castro's regime.

Among these ideas were that the US government would commit acts of aggression and even terrorism, and blame them on Castro to drum up support among the American public for a war with Cuba. Plans included:

• Disguising US planes as Cuban ones and having them attack military bases, such as Guantanamo, in Cuba itself. Then the reports would show that Cuban aircraft were to blame.

• Having those planes harass commercial airliners in US airspace, and attack shipping areas, causing genuine damage.

• Committing terrorist acts in Miami and even Washington, D.C., and planting evidence to show that Cuban revolutionaries were responsible. This would include bombings, the taking of hostages, and other acts that would unnerve the American public and make them feel outraged and unsafe.

• Attacking boats of Cuban refugees who were trying to escape from Cuba by sailing to Florida. The idea was to harass and maybe even injure some of them, without killing them, if possible. But such collateral damage couldn't be ruled out.

• Trying to provoke Cuba into taking actual military action, to frame the country as aggressive and in need of a US military response.

The whole point was to paint Cuba as a legitimate and immediate threat, so that the United States could have public support and the military could be authorized to use whatever force was necessary to stop Cuba. In short, these were "false flag" operations to frame Cuba.

This wasn't just some wild and fanciful idea promoted by one crank. The operation was taken seriously enough that the Joint Chiefs of Staff authorized it, and genuine plans were made for how to carry out these attacks. But President John F. Kennedy said no, and there is no evidence that any of the proposed attacks got beyond the idea stage. But some say that Kennedy's refusal to go along with the plan might have led to his assassination the following year.

For many 9/11 conspiracy theorists, the fact that the government was willing to attack and even kill its own people to frame a foreign power gave them further evidence that the events of that day were not what they seemed to be.

FEMA CONCENTRATION CAMPS

THE IDEA THAT THE US GOVERNMENT is secretly building dozens, if not hundreds, of concentration camps all around the United States is a very popular conspiracy theory in some circles, even though it seems pretty absurd on the face of it. In fact, some people claim that over 800 (!) of these camps already exist, and that they are masquerading as military bases, refugee centers, rescue centers for natural disasters, and so on. It's true, they say, that these places might really be used for such purposes . . . for now. But eventually, this oppressive and tyrannical government will strike against the "true Americans" and use these ready-made bases as detention centers and concentration camps for anyone who still tries to defend their liberties.

Obviously, this seems pretty ridiculous on the surface, but it's a theory that has many genuine believers, and disturbingly, the numbers are growing. It's very popular among militias and far right wing groups, who see it as only a matter of time before a tyrant declares martial law and starts to lock people away, or even kill them. A number of radio hosts, news personalities, podcasters, and other self-appointed experts seem to have jumped on the bandwagon for this idea and made it more popular among their listeners.

As proof, some theorists say that most of these hidden camps are in other facilities that are near railroad tracks and small airport runways. This will allow for large numbers of people to be transported to them when the time comes, and for military personnel to come and go easily. Also, many of them have sharp wire on the fences—further proof that these places will be used for keeping people in, not for keeping trespassers out. A retired police officer, Jack McLamb, claimed that Americans' mailboxes have already been secretly marked with distinct colored dots. Blue: the person will be taken to a concentration camp. Pink: the person will be arrested and made to do slave labor. Red: the person is to be shot and killed at once. This kind of nightmarishly paranoid thinking is hard to comprehend, but it has found favor on more than just fringe podcasts and websites.

Belief in it all goes back at least to the 1980s, when there were government talks about what to do in case of an emergency, such as a nuclear war, but the plans were never made official. At least, that's what the government wants you to think, according to FEMA camp believers. These camps already exist, they say, even though the evidence for them has always been shown to be misrepresentations, if not outright lies (an image of an alleged camp in Wyoming turned out to be a base in North Korea, for example). Further, no one has apparently ever escaped from one of these camps, and no one (such as an employee) has ever ratted one out.

That makes no difference to the true believers. Nothing will cause them to change their minds, and they will continue to spread this paranoid conspiracy with no regard for facts or evidence.

BLACK HELICOPTERS

THE STORY OF BLACK HELICOPTERS dates to the 1970s. People claimed to see black or dark-colored helicopters without any identifiable markings, often flying at low altitudes over populated areas. They weren't police or news copters, and they never seemed to do anything, just fly, hover, and maybe observe. Of course, as reports of these mysterious flying machines circulated, paranoia got ramped up and people began coming up with all kinds of creative ideas as to what they might be, who sent them, and what they were doing. Here is a look at some of the more popular conspiracy theories:

A military takeover: Quite a few theories have centered around how these craft are secret government flying machines, unmarked so that they cannot be identified. They are scouting out areas for population extermination or for laying out concentration camps, etc. This plan might have been implemented by the US government itself, but more likely, say believers, they are sent by the United Nations, to prepare the United States to submit to a one-world government headed by the UN. In the mid-1990s, some politicians took up the debate, claiming that unmarked helicopters were landing on ranch land to enforce environmental and other regulations. Militia groups have adopted some of these beliefs and still talk about them.

A sign of the end of the world: Some fundamentalist conspiracy theorists maintained that the mysterious craft were actually a sign of the end-time, as foretold in Revelation. Christian conspiracy theorist Hal Lindsey (author of *The Late Great Planet Earth*) offered the idea that these helicopters were actually described as locusts in the Book of Revelation, since the author of the book had obviously never seen one and wouldn't know what to call it. (None of Lindsey's other predictions ever came true, by the way, so we can probably discard this one.)

Part of the UFO phenomenon: Black helicopters allegedly have been seen in areas where there is heavy UFO activity, and in places where cattle mutilations have taken place. For many UFO believers, they are government vehicles scouting the area for clues, or are possibly trying to warn away anyone who is curious and gets too close. Some think that

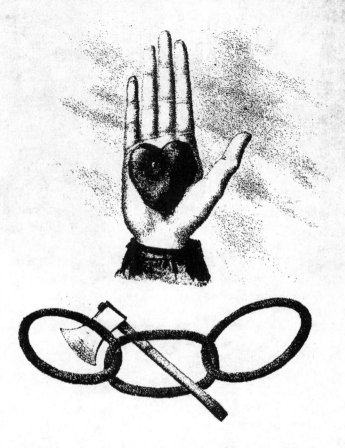

they might even be an illusion. A few witnesses have sworn that they have seen these helicopters transform into UFOs before flying off. Are they actually alien craft just messing with our minds?

Dark-colored helicopters have been used by various governmental organizations, such as the military and border patrol. For military usage, it is often to train pilots to fly in the dark without detection from the ground. Law enforcement agencies have used them while looking for smugglers and for narcotics patrols, among other things. Now, there are certainly concerns about civil liberties and citizens' rights that should be looked into when any military branch or police force uses unmarked craft, but these actual explanations are not nearly as exotic and strange as the conspiratorial ones.

THE OKLAHOMA CITY BOMBING

ON APRIL 19, 1995, a young, disgruntled veteran named Timothy McVeigh drove a Ryder truck filled with fertilizer explosives to a federal office building in Oklahoma City. The explosion destroyed the building, killing 168 people and wounding more than 600 others. It was a devastating attack that left the United States and the world in shock. McVeigh was arrested only about ninety minutes after the bombing, and he soon confessed to the attack, along with a coconspirator named Terry Nichols. McVeigh had been involved with antigovernment militias and groups, so it seemed pretty logical that he might have dreamed up the idea, especially in view of what had happened in Waco, Texas, two years earlier, when a botched government operation to remove a cult known as the Branch Davidians ended in tragedy and multiple deaths. McVeigh could have used that as an excuse to carry out his attack. But almost immediately, there were problems with his story. Here are some of the questions people have raised, which point to why quite a few people still think the case is not closed, and that cover-ups were involved:

• The attack was clearly well planned, so why did McVeigh try to get away in an old clunker of a car with no license plates? Looking as it did, he was bound to get pulled over by the police sooner or later. One answer is that this old car might have been intended to be left at the site as a clue or a "signature" for the bombing. If McVeigh decided to use it to get away, was he abandoned by other conspirators? If so, who were they?

• Nichols admitted that there were others involved in the plot; who were they? Amazingly, his statement never seems to have been properly investigated, or if it was, it was dropped.

• How did McVeigh and Nichols learn to build such powerful and damaging fertilizer bombs? They had no training, and it requires some specialized skills. Also, were there already bombs in the building? Some experts think so. If so, who put them there, and when?

• Over twenty eyewitnesses insisted that McVeigh was with other people the morning of the bombing; who were these people, and were they involved? No one has ever found out.

- At McVeigh's motel in Kansas before the bombing, he had rented a different Ryder truck. Why? And two days before the attack, who rented the actual truck that would carry the bombs, since this person didn't match McVeigh's description?

- There were a number of other possible suspects who might have been involved, but several of them seem to have never been questioned. Why were they not interrogated?

- The FBI learned that a far-right propagandist named Louis Beam had told an associate in 1994 that "something big" was going to happen on April 19, 1995, in either Oklahoma City, Dallas, or Denver. The FBI never interviewed him to find out more about what he knew. Why not?

Whatever McVeigh knew, he wasn't telling, and he took his secrets with him when he was executed for the crime on June 11, 2001. Some investigators think that this was a much larger operation, but the Clinton administration, still embarrassed about the disaster at Waco, wanted a quick win and conviction, and so they either dismissed valuable evidence, or never bothered to pursue certain lines of inquiry. Questions are still being asked.

THE 9/11 COVER-UP: THE ATTACKS

NO EVENT IN MODERN HISTORY has so polarized people of all political persuasions, or invited more conspiracy theories and alternate explanations than the terrorist attacks on September 11, 2001. Whole books can and have been written about 9/11 conspiracies, so this entry will be divided into three sections, focusing on a few aspects of that fateful day and the questions that still surround those terrible events.

Organizations and media such as *Popular Mechanics*, *NOVA*, the Smithsonian Channel, and the National Institute of Standards and Technology have all issued lengthy reports and documentaries debunking various 9/11 conspiracy theories. But so-called "truthers" have a seemingly endless number of theories and explanations for the events of that day. This first entry lists a few theories about the attacks themselves:

• The planes were hijacked, but flown remotely, and they already had explosives hidden on board. Some believe that this attack was too well coordinated and planned, and that there must have been more to it. They even say that there were no hijackers at all, and that the planes were flown by remote control, under the direction of unknown people. Some also believed that the hijackers were patsies, or actors. None of them could actually fly a plane, some theorists said, based on rumors of reports about how at least one of them had basically flunked out of the piloting school he was attending.

• A missile struck the Pentagon, not a plane. Some claimed that the lack of identifiable debris in the Pentagon itself proved that a plane had not struck the building at all, but rather that a guided missile had. They claimed that the plane seemed to simply disappear into the building, and that there was little evidence of wings or other parts of a commercial airliner; what was there was planted later. Further, some reported that security camera footage of the attack was captured by at least one gas station nearby, but this footage was confiscated by federal agents and has never been released to the public. But hundreds of eyewitnesses did indeed confirm that a plane flew into the Pentagon, so unless they were all actors or were warned to lie, it seems unlikely that something as visible as a missile attack in broad daylight would be misidentified.

• Flight 93, the fourth plane, was flying toward the White House or Capitol building, and was shot down by a missile. Believers in this theory say that it was not the passengers of Flight 93 that brought down the plane in an act of heroism, but instead the plane was destroyed by a missile to prevent another possible attack on Washington, D.C. In fact, an order had gone out to shoot the plane down, if necessary, to protect Washington, D.C., so in this instance, the conspiracy theorists might have a case. They have argued that it was shot down, and then the fact was covered up to avoid the backlash and anger that would undoubtedly come from taking such a drastic preemptive action.

THE 9/11 COVER-UP:
THE WORLD TRADE CENTER

THE TWO TOWERS were struck in succession and burned for some time before collapsing. The collapse of both buildings was horrifying and shocked viewers as they came crashing down, filling the air with ash and smoke and killing large numbers of people. But some viewers thought these collapses were very suspicious.

Several conspiracy theorists insisted that the way the towers fell looked much more like a controlled demolition than a response to airliners crashing into them. There was a regularity to the way the buildings fell, they said. It looked more like bombs had been placed on various floors and then detonated in succession, just as one would do to bring down an old and condemned building. This set off a wave of conspiracy theories, with reports of mysterious workers in the buildings in the weeks before the attacks, and people inside who survived saying that they heard explosions from within the buildings before they collapsed.

But experts in controlled demolition have pointed out that the way a building is brought down in such a demolition is by setting off explosives from the bottom and working up. In footage of the towers falling, windows can be seen blowing out as each floor collapses, which is essentially the opposite of what would happen in a controlled demolition. The intense heat from a jet explosion would be enough to weaken the structure and cause a collapse. Known as thermal expansion, the heat would have pressed the floors outward. The steel beams would have resisted this expansion. With nowhere to expand, the floors would have pulled the columns inward, causing them to buckle and collapse. The floors closest to the impact would go first, and their weight would fall on the floors below them, all the way down.

There was also a mystery surrounding the collapse of Building 7, which skeptics of the official explanation say shouldn't have happened at all. Building 7 was never hit by a plane, so why did it collapse? There were rumors that it was deliberately destroyed because it contained all kinds of incriminating information, and the destruction of the main towers

gave whoever wanted that information gone a chance to do so without obvious detection.

Part of this speculation came from an audio recording of someone saying "pull it," a term said to be used by firefighters when talking about deliberately destroying a building or other structure. So the theory up that bombs had been placed in that building, and that it was destroyed at the appropriate time. But further investigations showed that the fires from the Twin Towers had indeed spread to ten floors of Building 7, and that it was already in danger of collapsing. It collapsed about seven hours after the main buildings did, a long time to wait if it was being brought down deliberately.

THE 9/11 COVER-UP: RESPONSIBILITY

BLAME FOR THE ATTACKS BEGAN almost immediately. There were any number of suspects, from the likely to the very unlikely, and all of the accused have been studied exhaustively. While the evidence might point to a certain group of people, a single answer will never satisfy those who still see this era-defining event as being manipulated behind the scenes to push various agendas. Here are some of the main suspects:

Osama bin Laden and Al-Qaeda: Most consider bin Laden and Al-Qaeda to be the culprits behind the attacks. They point to previous attacks, such as on the USS *Cole* in 2000, and the earlier World Trade Center failed bombing in 1993, seeing these as trial runs for a much bigger operation. But not everyone believes this, of course.

Saddam Hussein and Iraq: Accusations of Saddam's involvement came almost immediately after the attacks, when he seemed to celebrate them. The idea that he was in league with Al-Qaeda and had a hand in the planning of the attacks was considered plausible at the time, and was even used by Bush administration officials, especially when argu-

ing for a new military offensive against Iraq. But later investigations revealed no proof that he was involved. Was he happy about the attacks? Probably, but he didn't seem to have anything to do with them.

Saudi Arabia: Noting that many of the hijackers were from Saudi Arabia, as was bin Laden himself, many wondered if that nation's government was involved in planning the attacks. Some became convinced that this was the case, but because Saudi Arabia is an ally of the United States and its oil supply is vital, the US government looked the other way when confronted with evidence of Saudi involvement.

The Bush administration: Many were not happy with the explanation that it was a simple case of a foreign terrorist power. They charged that these events and the legislation that came after them were all a little too convenient for pushing agendas that Bush's team wanted to push. Believers argued that high-ranking members of Bush's cabinet and possibly military members orchestrated these attacks, or at least let them happen, to help solidify their case to go to war in Iraq and Afghanistan.

They pointed to Operation Northwoods as an example of how it had already happened.

Israeli operatives: This action was allegedly to draw the United States into greater conflict in the Middle East. Rumors that several thousand Jewish people stayed home that day—because they were tipped off by Mossad, Israel's intelligence service—have since been proven false.

The Bilderbergers or bankers: The idea that a secretive banking or finance group may have planned the attacks was appealing for some. There is a lot of money to be made in war, and getting the United States involved in a multiyear conflict was certainly good for business. Some pointed to curious activity in the stock market on September 10 as proof that someone well positioned knew what was going to happen, and was preparing for the market to go into chaos the next day.

The Illuminati or other secretive group: According to this theory, 9/11 was another in a long line of incidents meant to bring people under further control and restrict freedom. Some saw this as proof that the Illuminati (or some other group) was manipulating world events to rob people of their freedom, by making them scared and compliant. The Patriot Act and other restrictive laws in the United States were further proof of this.

THE SANDY HOOK COVER-UP AND THE "FALSE FLAG" THEORY

THE SHOOTINGS AT SANDY HOOK ELEMENTARY SCHOOL in Newtown, Connecticut, on December 14, 2012, shocked America and the world. A young gunman first killed his mother, then went to the school and killed six staff members, twenty schoolchildren, and, finally, himself. It was an appalling tragedy that outraged people of all political beliefs. But for some, there was more to the situation than met the eye.

As offensive as it might seem, within days—if not hours—of the shootings, stories started circulating about how all was not as it appeared.

One of the main theories was that the shootings did not happen. Or rather, that no one died. The whole thing was a training exercise by the Department of Homeland Security. Others claimed that the murders did happen, but that the shooter was under some kind of mind control (MK-Ultra still up and running, perhaps), and did things he would never have done otherwise. Again, this was to advance a secret agenda. An anti-Semitic take on the shooting was broadcast in Iran and elsewhere, saying that the shooting was done by "Israeli death squads." This theory was taken up by neo-Nazi groups and other far-right organizations as proof that the Jews were trying to strike terror into the hearts of Americans.

You might think that these are very ugly and cynical views of a terrible tragedy, and you'd be right. Proponents of these fringe theories, like

Alex Jones, have made outlandish claims about "crisis actors" with no proof at all, as did conspiracy theorist James Tracy. Tracy implied that child actors had been hired from Colorado's Visionbox Studio Theatre, and that the whole Sandy Hook tragedy was staged (see the next entry for more on crisis actors).

Both Tracy and Jones said that the massacre of children was faked by the government for various reasons. It was a "false flag" operation to advance stronger gun control legislation, or even a move to repeal the Second Amendment of the US Constitution (the one guaranteeing the right to bear arms). But it was all for a secret agenda. The children were not dead, and even their parents were in on it.

Finally, outraged and grief-stricken parents of the dead children had enough of Jones's lies and took him to court over his false claims. In October 2021, the court ruled in their favor, an important and strong statement about how far one can go when making up outrageous stories. Free speech does not protect one from the consequences of that speech, and the court recognized this important distinction. The tragedy of Sandy Hook really happened, and all the theorizing about hidden motivations for it cannot erase that fact.

CRISIS ACTORS

YOU'VE LIKELY HEARD this term bandied about at one time or another, often after a mass shooting, a terrorist attack, or even a natural disaster. While it means something very different to people who use the term in those cases, crisis actors are real, and they serve a useful purpose. Real crisis actors are, indeed, trained actors who take on the roles of disaster victims. Their purpose is to help train first responders: the police, firefighters, the National Guard, and other rescue professionals. In training missions, crisis actors have a valuable part to play in giving needed experience to those who will all too soon have to go out and do it for real. They can play victims with various injuries, and will even wear realistic makeup to simulate cuts, burns, and so on. They give first responders of all kinds the needed practice so that when a real crisis comes, they can be ready.

But for certain conspiracy theorists, crisis actors are something completely different, something sinister. For them, crisis actors are part of a plot, usually hatched by the government. When something like a mass shooting happens, some conspiracy theorists will insist that it never happened at all, and that the so-called victims are actually actors paid to pretend that they have been wounded or killed. The witnesses are also actors, claiming to have seen horrors that never happened.

Why would these people participate in this? The usual explanation is that the government is trying to impose some new draconian law: gun control, extra surveillance, or new restrictions on civil liberties. The idea is that each time one of these crimes is said to happen, it allows the government to tighten its grip on power. They are elaborate fakes meant to fool people into giving up their own power in order to feel safer.

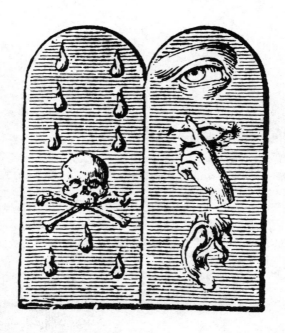

The Sandy Hook shooting was one example of this ugly conspiracy theory, but there are many others, and often theorists try to link several events into one big conspiracy. This might be a grand government or UN conspiracy to take away people's rights and sovereignty, but sometimes believers in the bizarre will tip over into the supernatural as the best explanation. Some claim that mass shootings and even natural disasters are part of occult or satanic conspiracies. Using black magic, practitioners are able to "conjure" up bad weather, but this demands "sacrifices." Okay, but what about the so-called crisis actors? Well, this is where it all gets pretty convoluted and nonsensical. Some of these things are staged to bring about general unease, and then the satanic-induced disasters bring the real death. Or maybe they don't, and those are all crisis actors, too. It's a mess.

But the idea that actors are pretending to be victims in order to advance some secret agenda is pretty silly and even offensive, and causes even more pain to those who are already suffering.

THE BARACK OBAMA "BIRTHER" CONSPIRACY THEORY

THIS CONSPIRACY THEORY came about when Barack Obama first ran for president in the 2008 election, though it persists even today. People who were opposed to him (some hard-core conservatives, as well as racists) started spreading the story that he was actually ineligible to run for president at all because he was not a natural-born citizen of the United States, which is required by Article II of the Constitution. So, they argued, he should not be able to run. They insisted that he had not been born in Hawaii, as he claimed, but in Kenya. Others claimed that he had given up his US citizenship to become an Indonesian citizen, and was therefore also ineligible that way.

This idea was taken up by Donald Trump, among others, who claimed to have evidence that Obama was lying about his citizenship. People started demanding that Obama produce his birth certificate to prove that he was actually born in Hawaii. On June 12, 2008, the Obama campaign released a scan of his 1961 birth certificate on a website called "Fight the Smears." If they hoped that this would settle the issue, they were very wrong. Almost immediately, conspiracy theorists insisted that the birth certificate was fake, altered, Photoshopped, or whatever else they could think of.

In April 2011, the Obama White House obtained copies of the so-called "long-form" birth certificate, and certified copies of the original Certificate of Live Birth, in order to show them to the press and put an end to the controversy once and for all. Examination of these documents showed them to be authentic and that he was indeed born in Hawaii on August 4, 1961. And again, conspiracy theorists weren't satisfied. They insisted that it was a forgery made with image editing software. In short, nothing was going to be good enough for them.

The whole thing should have been laughable, but the number of media personalities and even politicians who took it seriously showed that there was still a serious problem in the United States with racism and mistrust. Many compared the whole thing to the "show your papers"

demands that so many African Americans had endured over the twentieth century. Further, no white presidential candidate (Republican or Democrat) had ever been asked to prove that they were an American citizen before. The whole thing smacked of racism to a lot of observers, and showed just how much work still needed to be done.

Ultimately, the story wasn't enough to put off his supporters, and Obama won two presidential terms. But even years later, polls showed that significant numbers of Republican voters still believed that he wasn't born in the United Sates, despite all the evidence to the contrary. And that shows the power of a belief and how hard it is to dislodge it when it gets into someone's head.

QANON

QANON IS A RECENT DEVELOPMENT in the ever-growing world of conspiracy theories. Only a few years old, it has grown into a large (bloated, even) set of beliefs that includes just about everything you can think of, all wrapped up in one oversized package. It's popular with those on the far right, and has support among a good number of Trump supporters. Polls have shown that up to 17 percent of Americans believe at least the basic parts of the conspiracy theory, but it has grown into such a massive set of ideas and conspiracies that it's difficult to keep track of it.

At its core, the QAnon conspiracy started in October 2017, on the message board 4chan. A user with the name "Q Clearance Patriot" posted, claiming to be a high-ranking government official or insider who had special knowledge about classified information. "Q" claimed that Donald Trump was clandestinely waging a war against a corrupt cabal that was secretly running the world, like the Illuminati or another shadowy organization. This cabal includes many familiar faces, including Hillary Clinton, Barack Obama, Joe Biden, and George Soros; celebrities such as

Tom Hanks and Oprah Winfrey; and spiritual leaders such as the Dalai Lama and the pope.

The group worships Satan and engages in rituals involving pedophilia, human sacrifice, and cannibalism. They eat their victims to absorb a chemical called adrenochrome, which they believe extends their lives. Trump, so the theory goes, was recruited by top military leaders to run for president, and is waging a covert war against this cabal. Soon, these monsters will be arrested and executed, and America will be restored to true greatness.

At the conspiracy's core, these ideas seem pretty outlandish and bizarre, but since its birth, it has grown to include many other conspiracy theories, including alternate theories about the assassination of John F. Kennedy, as well as support for the 9/11 "truther" movement. Beginning in 2021, the movement has also strongly supported the idea that Joe Biden stole the 2020 presidential election. But it's the satanic, cannibal pedophiles who have captured the imagination of its many believers.

Q's identity is a mystery. Some speculate that it may be more than one person, while others think it really is from one government insider. Q's frequency of posting has dropped off since the 2020 election, but that hasn't lessened the movement, and a remarkable number of people seem to believe in it, as preposterous as it seems. Once only believed by those on the far right, some evangelicals have embraced the ideas, as have some who might be considered much more left-leaning in their views (health gurus and New Age teachers, for example). No amount of debunking or arguing will change their minds.

Social media has played a big role in spreading the conspiracy, and while sites like Facebook and YouTube have banned QAnon pages on their platforms, many see it as too little, too late. And while none of Q's predictions about mass arrests and executions have happened, the followers don't care; they simply reinterpret those confusing messages to mean something else, which is a convenient way of avoiding thinking about being wrong. While many see Q as nothing more than a hoaxer who got away with fooling a lot of people, it remains to be seen how the whole thing will play out. Some of the most devoted followers have

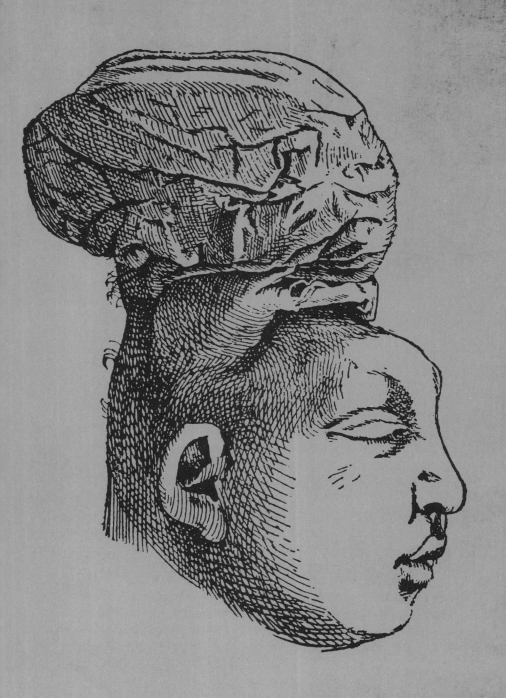

already threatened acts of violence or even committed them, and that has a lot of people worried.

THE "DEEP STATE"

THE "DEEP STATE" is a kind of umbrella term that can mean differ-ent things to different people, and so it is a good entry to close out this section. While most popular with those on the right, it can also be used by left-wing thinkers or anyone who thinks that there is more going on in our government and daily lives than we actually see. Simply defined, the "deep state" refers to the idea that a group of unelected political and military officials, as well as financial bigwigs, are able to secretly influ-ence US policy, regardless of who is the president. They have an agenda of their own, and don't care about Republicans or Democrats; they only care about advancing their own goals. On several occasions, beginning in 2017, Donald Trump claimed that deep-state operatives were inter-fering with his agenda. These operatives were Democrats with their own plans, he said, and Trump played up this idea to his supporters.

Some argue that the "deep state" is really just the entrenched bureau-cracy of the United States, and as such it has existed for a very long time. What seems like conspiracies to undermine presidents or Con-gress is more likely just a government that moves slowly and often resists change. This, they say, is essential to the functioning of the US government, to ensure that certain institutions continue, regardless of who is in office, or which party controls the Senate and the House. Bureaucracy is not conspiracy; it's simply necessary for something as complex as a government to function.

But, of course, some conspiracy theorists wanted to jump on the bandwagon and promote the idea of an unhinged deep state that had been manipulating events for decades, if not centuries. In this, the deep state isn't much different from the Illuminati or the Masons; it's just an updated version of older ideas. Alex Jones tried to tie the concept of the deep state to events like the Oklahoma City bombing, the Sandy Hook massacre, and even the bombing at the Boston Marathon. All of these were events orchestrated by the deep state to further its own agenda and tighten its control over the American people.

As we've seen, the notion of a secret society controlling the world as its puppet master is not new. While some have expressed legitimate worries that certain portions of the US government do not have enough oversight and might be able to act on their own in some ways, most political scientists dismiss the idea of an all-encompassing and controlling "deep state" as the product of overactive imaginations and the never-ending appeal of conspiracy-theory thinking.

De Weght tot CHRISTU

Math: 11 ꝟ 12

CHAPTER 5
SECRET & MYSTERIOUS LOCATIONS

WHO DOESN'T LOVE a place shrouded in mystery? Whether it's a haunted house, an old mine, or a secret meeting place, we're drawn to places that might be more than they seem. Are they locations where clandestine groups get together? Do they contain unknown, priceless treasures? Do they hold secrets that the world can never know about? Are they natural formations that conceal terrible secrets about our planet's fate? Or maybe their existence is just a rumor, and they don't exist at all?

For almost any kind of place, there is probably a conspiracy theory to go with it. This chapter looks at some of the more fantastic and unusual places around the world that have fired people's imaginations and led them to think that there might be more than meets the eye in these

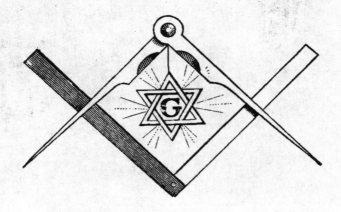

DENVER INTERNATIONAL AIRPORT

AN AIRPORT MIGHT SEEM LIKE a bit of a strange place for a whole group of elaborate conspiracy theories to grow up around, but that's just what has happened with Denver International Airport. What's so interesting about an airport, other than that it's a place to get to and from other places? Well, devotees of the Denver Airport conspiracies have quite an interesting story to tell. . . .

The airport is relatively new, only being opened in 1995. It is characterized by unusual architecture, design, and decoration, an odd runway configuration, and underground tunnels, all of which have driven conspiracy theorists wild with speculation. Plus, the current management seems keen to encourage conspiracy talk, as a way of drumming up more business. Here is a selection of what believers have come up with:

The Masons, or the Illuminati, or the New World Order, are behind the funding, construction, and running of the airport. One or more of these secret societies are behind the whole thing, from the design to the actual construction, and they've left numerous clues around, hinting at their involvement. Why would they do that? Because they're arrogant and think they can get away with it, of course. Thankfully, the conspiracy theorists see through their clever plans!

It contains strange art and languages that hint at a coming apocalypse. The airport displays murals by artist Leo Tanguma, which depict a number of disturbing scenes of war and fascism, but which, when viewed as a whole, express the hope for peace and a healed environment. A giant mustang sculpture outside supposedly represents the Four Horsemen of the Apocalypse . . . or maybe it's just a horse. The airport has various gargoyles leering out of walls, but anyone who knows a bit about their history knows that gargoyles were placed on buildings as waterspouts and to protect against evil. And those "alien" languages and symbols? Navajo.

It has underground tunnels leading to alien and/or Nazi bases. The airport has underground baggage transport tunnels to make getting luggage to and from airplanes efficient (as do most airports). But rumors have circulated that there is something under these tunnels, something sinister, whether it's a secret alien or Nazi base, or a bunker for the elite to retreat to in the event of an apocalypse. Believers will tell you there is definitely something down there. But various tours have shown how difficult it would be to have placed anything else under those tunnels. Still, some employees have donned lizard and alien masks as a prank.

The runways are shaped like a swastika. Maybe, kind of, sort of, if you really try hard? It's actually a fan design that allows for the best takeoffs and landings in a windy area. If you've ever flown into or out of Denver Airport, you know how windy it can get! The runways were designed to help with this.

These are some of the biggies, but there are others. The fact is that it takes a good bit of imagination to make any of these things even a little bit plausible, and the truth is usually far more boring, sorry to say!

MOUNT RUSHMORE'S
"HIDDEN" CHAMBER

MOUNT RUSHMORE IN SOUTH DAKOTA is a world-famous monument that is seen by some as an amazing work of art and testimony to the spirit of America, while others see it as more evidence of colonial attitudes and taking native lands without permission to install symbols of that oppression. But we're not here to get into that debate. Whatever one's opinion of the monument, there is a curious fact about it that many people know little or nothing about: the secret chamber located behind it.

Well, it's not all that "secret." It was a pet project of one of the designers and sculptors, Gutzon Borglum. In addition to very grand plans for the front surface, Borglum wanted to design a chamber behind the famous faces that would be a "hall of records" for important US documents—everything from the Constitution to significant artifacts and objects. They could be safely held there, and brought out from time to time for public viewing.

The problem, of course, was that the project started to get away from the designers, and they had issues with the money the government had allocated for it. So, some of the more elaborate plans had to be set aside. Still, things progressed nicely, and by 1941, the work was nearly complete. Unfortunately, Borglum died just before the job was finished, and the task fell to his son, Lincoln, who completed his father's vision. But he didn't have the funding or the energy to work on his father's plan for a full "secret" chamber.

The government officials were disappointed that work on the chamber had ended, and the project was scrapped. Or was it? The beginnings of the hall that would have led to the chamber were open to the public for some time, but now no longer are. Even more suspiciously (at least according to some people), the government placed a huge slab of granite (weighing over 1,200 tons) over the entrance, to make sure that no one could enter the hall. Now that doesn't sound questionable, does it?

So why did the government seal it off? What's back there that they don't want people seeing? Or what are they doing that they don't want the public to know about? The real answer is probably nothing at all, but that hasn't stopped conspiracy theorists from speculating wildly about what might be going on in there. Was the chamber actually completed in secret? Is there another hidden entrance?

Believers say that the government is hiding important classified information back there, or maybe vast amounts of wealth (such as Templar treasure), or even proof of alien life; there is something there that someone doesn't want the American people to know about. Why it would be there, no one can explain, but why let logic get in the way of a good theory? In fact, it looks like a portion of the hall was used in the past to store fireworks for Fourth of July celebrations, so there's that, at least!

THE SAFEGUARD COMPLEX

A PYRAMID WITH ITS POINTY TOP cut off sits way out in the middle of nowhere in North Dakota. And that's pretty much all you need to know to understand why conspiracy believers are so interested in it. It's actually part of the Stanley R. Mickelsen Safeguard Complex, which was designed as an antiballistic missile system in the bad old days of the Cold War. The chopped-off pyramid was supposed to be part of a radar system to warn of incoming missiles from the Soviet Union or China, and also mount a defense against them. The project was approved in 1969, and construction began in 1970.

The complex was opened on October 1, 1975. The very next day, the US House of Representatives voted to close it, though it continued to operate until February 10, 1976. For some conspiracy believers, this action immediately set off alarm bells. Why would the government authorize an expensive system like this, take five years to build it, and then shut it down right away?

It turned out that a lot of representatives were not thrilled with the project or the cost to get it up and running, and there were concerns about agreements with the Soviets, and how this complex might be endangering treaties. So, to be on the safe side, various officials decided to close the whole thing down, rather than risk losing more money or causing an international incident. It turned out that the Soviets were impressed with the site, and the United States might have designed it as a way of showing off its power and bargaining with the USSR. If so, it worked.

The lonely pyramid still stands today, a reminder of a long-ago time when two superpowers competed against each other, using the world like a chessboard. But what if it was more than that? What if someone else ordered the pyramid to be built? What if that someone was . . . the Illuminati? For conspiracy theorists, the whole thing is just so obvious. The pyramid with the top cut off looks very much like the "Eye of Providence" on the back of the US $1 bill, and this image has long been known to be a Masonic symbol; many of this country's founders were Freemasons, after all. Is it possible that the Safeguard Complex is really a Masonic/Illuminati headquarters, one that was seemingly abandoned in 1976, but which has served as a place where this secretive group can draw up its dastardly plans in secret?

Well, maybe. But what would be the point of advertising their location, remote though it is, with a big symbol? A secret society that puts up a massive building using one of its supposed symbols isn't doing a very good job of being "secret." It would be rather like a comic-book supervillain, putting a sign on their lair, advertising it as "Supervillain Headquarters." Realistically, the Safeguard Complex probably really is just what the government says it is: an abandoned military base from a different time.

THE SECRET CHAMBER
UNDER THE SPHINX

THE SPHINX STANDS (or rather, sits) mysteriously at the Plateau of Giza in Egypt, just as famous, if not even more, than the nearby pyramids. For a lot of people, it's the most recognizable symbol of ancient Egypt. And for many, it hides secrets which could be truly stunning and change our whole view of the world and history.

First, there is evidence that it might be much older than the ancient Egyptians. A geologist named Robert M. Schoch was able to demonstrate years ago that the monument shows evidence of being weathered and worn down by rain over a very long period of time. Now, as you know, Egypt is a pretty hot and dry country, and it was just as hot and dry during the age of the pharaohs, so how could it be rain weathered? Well, if you go back farther in time, say between 5,000 and 7,000 BCE, there was indeed a lot of rain in the area, which would have been enough to carve marks in the stone.

So, some people believe that a previously unknown people or civilization might have fashioned it first, and that it was later taken over and redone by the Egyptians. This is a hotly debated topic, and shows no signs of being settled soon. But for some believers, this is proof of the claims of an American psychic and prophet named Edgar Cayce, who maintained that before the Egyptians, survivors of Atlantis had escaped doom and built a new civilization at the site, about 12,000 years ago. He said there was a "hall of records" under the Sphinx that held the proof of this long-lost civilization.

The thing is, there do seem to be tunnels under the Sphinx, but excavation and careful drilling have not yet turned up a hall of records. It seems that these small tunnels might lead to natural caves, but there is also some evidence that there might be carved chambers under the monument. Is one of these Cayce's fabled hall of records? Believers say yes, but further excavations are unlikely, in order to preserve the stone.

Conspiracy theorists think that the Egyptian government and others already know what's down there, and maybe have even removed it for study, but, of course, they don't want to tell the world, because it would overturn pretty much everything we think we know about history, prove that Atlantis existed, and show that Cayce was right. It seems that the riddle of the Sphinx is still waiting to be solved.

THE GEORGIA GUIDESTONES

THIS MYSTERIOUS MONUMENT in the state of Georgia has caused strong opinions all around. Unlike a lot of monuments, this one is pretty recent, and was built deliberately to be put in Elbert County. In 1979, a man using the name R. C. Christian asked a granite company to construct the monument for him. The company said no, but Christian was willing to pay more than their price, saying that he represented a secret group that had wanted the monument built for twenty years. The monument was built, and it was unveiled to curious onlookers in March 1980.

It consists of a series of standing stones, Stonehenge-like in appearance, but carved with writing. One slab is in the center, with four around it, forming an X, and a capstone stands on top of them. They are aligned astronomically. A nearby stone explains their purpose: "Let these be guidestones to an Age of Reason."

There are instructions on the main four slabs, written in eight modern languages (English, Spanish, Russian, Hebrew, Arabic, Swahili, Hindi, and Chinese):

1. Maintain humanity under 500,000,000 in perpetual balance with nature.

2. Guide reproduction wisely—improving fitness and diversity.

3. Unite humanity with a living new language.

4. Rule passion—faith—tradition—and all things with tempered reason.

5. Protect people and nations with fair laws and just courts.

6. Let all nations rule internally, resolving external disputes in a world court.

7. Avoid petty laws and useless officials.

8. Balance personal rights with social duties.

9. Prize truth—beauty—love—seeking harmony with the infinite.

10. Be not a cancer on the Earth—leave room for nature—leave room for nature.

Shorter messages are also carved in four ancient languages (Babylonian/cuneiform, Egyptian hieroglyphs, Sanskrit, and Classical Greek).

While some see these writings as a call to reason and rationality, some Christian conspiracy theorists have denounced the monument, labeling the words "the ten commandments of the Antichrist," or instructions for a Devil-worshipping sun cult. Some have demanded that the stones be destroyed, saying they reveal the plans of a satanic cult to cull the Earth of most human beings and usher in a new age of "godlessness."

One theory was that the builders feared imminent destruction in a nuclear war (the Cold War was still dragging on when the monument was unveiled), and wanted to provide instructions to the survivors on how to rebuild civilization. R. C. Christian, so the theory goes, instructed the builders to make sure that the stones could remain standing in case of a disaster.

As for the identity of the person who had them built? No one knows, but some have seen his name as a clue: "R. C. Christian" could mean "Rose Cross" Christian, or Christian Rosenkreuz. Remember him? He was the legendary founder of the Rosicrucian Order. So is this a Rosicrucian monument, erected to announce to the world that the order is still around and keeping an eye on things? Or maybe it was just an expensive prank? Why choose Elbert County? No one really knows for sure why the stones are there, and the builders aren't talking.

THE NAZIS HAD A BASE
IN ANTARCTICA

IT'S NO SECRET THAT HITLER wanted every advantage he could get, even those from unconventional sources. While the Nazis publicly condemned occultism and banned various groups, it's widely believed that at least some of them in secret were searching for supernatural help, everything from the Spear of Destiny (the legendary weapon that pierced the side of Christ) to the Ark of the Covenant and the Holy Grail (as Indiana Jones could tell you!), to searching for the entry at the North Pole into a hollow Earth, to summoning demons, to just about anything else you can think of.

One of the more interesting theories is that the Nazis had a base at Antarctica. The origins of this story do have a basis in truth. From December 1938 to April 1939, a German ship, MS *Schwabenland*, did sail to Antarctica on a mission to claim a portion of the continent and protect Germany's whaling interests. But the outbreak of the war prevented any further expeditions, as Germany turned its attention to trying to conquer the world, not just the southern continent. At least, that's the story everyone tells. But according to some, there was something much

bigger and more involved going on in Antarctica: the Nazis were building a secret base. This base, they say, was completed, but in the 1950s
was destroyed by a nuclear weapon and buried.

That's quite a story, but what was going on there? Well, one version ties
back into the belief that Hitler didn't die, but escaped from Germany
(see the Historical Conspiracies chapter). In this version, Hitler did
not escape to South America, but he and Eva Braun were brought to
the secret base in Antarctica. In July 1945, a German U-boat, the *U-530*,
showed up at the Argentine naval base at Mar del Plata. For later theorists, this was proof that it had secretly taken Hitler and his entourage
away from Germany—and not just Hitler, but whole teams of Nazis scientists, military commanders, and others. From their secret base, they
continued with their plans, seeing their situation as only a temporary
setback and eventually perfecting the flying discs that would become
the UFOs spotted in the 1950s.

The Allied powers, aware of what was going on, finally located the
base and nuked it in 1958. It turns out that there were US nuclear tests
north of Antarctica in August and September of that year, but they were
nowhere near where the base was supposed to have been, or really all
that close to Antarctica to begin with.

Other, wilder versions of the theory suggest that the Nazis had made
an agreement with a group of aliens, who would supply them with
alien tech (for the flying saucers) and continue to support them if they
won the war. When the Nazis were trounced, the aliens withdrew their
support and decided to test the Americans instead, manufacturing the
famed crash at Roswell to see how the US military and government
would react.

Getting back to the main theory, the area where the Nazi base was supposed to have stood has been explored extensively by multiple scientific
missions (for reasons other than looking for a Nazi base), and no one
has ever reported anything unusual. Unless, of course, they're all in on
the conspiracy to keep it a secret . . .

A SUPERVOLCANO UNDER YELLOWSTONE

SCIENTISTS KNOW THAT THERE IS A LOT of volcanic activity under Yellowstone National Park in the United States. Yellowstone is a huge tourist attraction, because of its geysers and hot springs, including its famous Old Faithful geyser. And that's the whole issue: that heat all has to come from somewhere. The reason the water is so hot is that it's being heated under the Earth in a very geologically active area. And why is it so active? Because Yellowstone is on top of what geologists lovingly call a "supervolcano." These kinds of volcanoes are not your usual run-of-the-mill mountains that spew lava. Oh no, when they erupt, they are absolutely devastating. As pressure builds up under the Earth and is not released, it can trigger a full-scale eruption from a giant, underground volcano filled with lava. These eruptions can spew endless amounts of rock and ash into the sky, and destroy everything around them.

The last time the Yellowstone supervolcano erupted was about 664,000 years ago, and it left a depression/crater that was thirty-four by fifty miles wide. Known as the Yellowstone Caldera, we can still see it today. Another eruption like that now would be almost unthinkable. It would destroy everything for hundreds of miles, spew ash over most of the United States and beyond, and change the world's weather for a decade or more, given all the pollutants that it would eject into the atmosphere. It would be truly apocalyptic and might end civilization as we know it.

Scary stuff! But how likely is it to happen again anytime soon? Well, according to the US Geological Survey, it's not likely at all, at least for 100,000 more years. In any case, it might never erupt like that again, but instead might let off much smaller eruptions that will do far less damage.

But if you listen to some conspiracy theorists, that's not true at all. They say that the government has a sense of when the supervolcano will erupt again, and is hiding that information to prevent a public panic, because it will happen soon. Some have said that scientists would have about two months' notice before a major eruption, and that US policy is already in place to say nothing beforehand, because it would be easier to let people die and clean up afterward that it would be to evacuate

everyone out of the danger zone (which could be hundreds of thousands, even millions, of people). So the government already plans to let everyone in the area die, and it has a decent idea of when the volcano will erupt again.

This seems like a very cynical and dark belief, even as far as conspiracy theories go! Fortunately, in addition to the USGS, a good number of scientists have come forward to show that the volcano won't be bursting out anytime soon, which makes the whole conspiratorial policy of secrecy about impending destruction a nonissue, anyway.

THE LOUISIANA SINKHOLE

ONE NIGHT IN AUGUST 2012, the ground near the Louisiana town of Bayou Corne started to shake and rumble. To everyone's surprise, a gigantic sinkhole began to open in the ground, forcing the town to evacuate. The sinkhole has grown since then, getting bigger every year. Naturally, residents are confused and angry. What is going on?

Well, it turns out the area was being mined by a petrochemical company called Texas Brine. The company uses a process called injection mining, where they sink wells into a giant salt dome under the earth and pump out saltwater, from which the salt is extracted and used for commercial purposes. It seemed pretty obvious that the company probably drilled too much, or too deep, weakened the geology of the area, and caused a massive sinkhole to open up. Of course, in typical corporate-speak, Texas Brine didn't really take any responsibility, preferring to talk about how "safe" their operations were, and so on.

Still, angry residents and the state government got after them and told them to clean up what they could or be shut down, so Texas Brine complied. But there's not much they can do at this point, as the sinkhole continues to grow and probably will for a while.

But those who claim to be in the know think that there is more to this story than mere corporate corruption and greed leading to a disaster. They think it shows worrying signs of a much bigger collapse. The theory is that these kinds of weak spots along fault lines underground actually extend all the way into the Gulf of Mexico, where they can be observed on the seafloor. This sinkhole might have been caused by a mining mistake, but that made things much worse, since it will start to weaken other areas all the way down into the Gulf. When they weaken too much, they will collapse, just as the area around Bayou Corne did. And when that happens, much of Louisiana and its neighboring states will collapse into the Gulf, killing untold millions of people and burying New Orleans and other cities underwater forever.

And, of course, corporations and the government already know this, but are keeping it secret to avoid a public panic, and, because it's just not possible to evacuate everyone from the danger zones (just like with Yellowstone). The government figures it's easier to let the area disappear and for all those people to die, and deal with the impact of everything later. So, as with Yellowstone, a catastrophe is waiting to happen, and there's nothing anyone can do about it. If you live in New Orleans, you can sleep better, knowing that!

FINLAND DOESN'T EXIST

OKAY, THIS ONE IS JUST STRAIGHT-UP WEIRD. How can somebody just make up a whole country? Well, for Finland (and Australia; see the next entry), some conspiracy theorists believe that it's true. This idea actually seems to have started over on Reddit back in 2014, when someone posted about how their parents never believed Finland existed, and the poster grew up thinking this too, until they did some research and found out that their parents were wrong. Apparently, the parents believed that "Finland" was just a part of eastern Sweden, so people who claimed to be visiting a country called Finland were just in Sweden without realizing it. There is really just a big body of water there, an extension of the Baltic Sea.

Why would anyone believe something like this? Well, according to this poster, the hoax of a country called Finland was actually invented by the Soviet Union and Japan, working together. The concept that a whole country could be invented is so weird that no one would ever doubt the country actually exists, and the UN is keeping the secret. But why?

Well, it has to do with Japan wanting to be able to fish more than they are allowed to under international law. Since there is actually a big mass of water where Finland should be, they are able to fish there in secret and not be subject to any regulations. They then ship the fish back through Russia on a trans-Siberian train and deliver it to Japan. Russia gets to keep a portion of the fish for itself, for providing this secret assistance. The "Finnish" phone company Nokia is actually owned by Japan, you see, and yes, some argue that the name even sounds Japanese. But why the name "Finland"? Because fish have fins, so the inside joke is that there is a "land" full of finned fish, i.e., it's just water.

Yes, it's bizarre, it's ridiculous, and most people see it as nothing more than a silly hoax, even if the original poster's parents really did believe it (and who knows if that's actually true?). The internet being the internet, there are always going to be at least a few people who take any idea seriously, and get mad if you try to point out how absurd the whole thing is. People from Finland will be happy to confirm that they and their country really exist, but, of course, they're just Swedish conspirators in on the plot too. . . .

AUSTRALIA DOESN'T EXIST

AH, ANOTHER COUNTRY THAT DOESN'T EXIST! But unlike the joke about Finland's nonexistence, one group of people, the Flat Earthers (more about them in the next chapter), are quite convinced that the whole continent of Australia is nothing but an elaborate hoax. People who visit are not actually flying there, you see. They are being secretly rerouted to South America, and are led to believe that they are in Australia, in order to preserve the fiction that the world is round. You can see why these people start giving scientists a headache after a while.

But Australia as a fictional country, they say, goes back to Britain in the nineteenth century. Since the continent was allegedly originally set up as a penal colony, a place where the Victorians could send all their criminals, it was seen as an "out of sight, out of mind" solution. But those who believe differently say that the real story is far more sinister. The Victorians weren't sending criminals to "Australia," they say. No, they were executing them, by the thousands, and covering it up by pretending to ship them off to a new land on the other side of the world, where they could serve their time and then maybe start new lives.

Now, this is bizarre enough, of course, but some believers in a flat Earth think it's even worse. They didn't execute these criminals in secret by hanging them or by firing squad. No, they really did put them on ships to sail to a land they called Australia. But what happened was that these ships reached the edge of the flat Earth and fell over the edge, basically killing everyone on board. We can assume that the ships' captains and crews abandoned ship long before the edge and left the criminals to fend for themselves.

This brings up a whole lot of other problems, such as, why doesn't all the water just drain off the edge of the Earth? Also, many Flat Earthers believe that the entire disc of the Earth is surrounded by ice—what we call Antarctica—so if that's the case, how did these ships simply fall off the edge? Or maybe the criminals were left at the ice to fend for themselves, and they all died? Unfortunately, logic is not a strong point for people who are really into this stuff.

As with the Finns, there are a whole lot of Aussies who are either amused or upset by the news that they don't exist, and have spoken up about it in comments online. It makes for a great joke and satire, but the fact is, there are people out there who really believe that Australia doesn't exist, and that visitors are just going somewhere in South America and seeing actors pretending to be Aussies. It's hard to imagine the mental gymnastics needed to believe something like this!

CHAPTER 6
SCIENTIFIC CONSPIRACIES

SCIENTIFIC CONSPIRACIES are probably just as hot a topic as political ones these days. Over the last century and more, people have looked to scientists for answers and explanations, but increasingly, some people reject those scientific answers and see scientists as part of the problem in keeping people ignorant and under the control of the powerful. It's an unfortunate situation, but it's one that's growing, and it's an issue that needs to be addressed by the scientific community. When they are seen as elites who are "out of touch" with people who would rather get their information from online videos, it can lead to all sorts of problems.

This chapter looks at a whole host of scientific conspiracies, from rumors of hidden health cures and suppressed technologies to the classic claim that the moon landings were faked, to more modern theories such as that we're all living in a computer simulation (which, to be honest, is not impossible, according to the math). The one takeaway from these ideas, whether possible or wacky, is that scientific literacy is needed now more than ever.

RFID CHIPS

RADIO FREQUENCY IDENTIFICATION, or RFID, is all the rage among conspiracy theorists these days. The idea is pretty simple and pretty sinister: this technology can be put into small chips, which can then be embedded in things (including humans!), allowing them to be tracked and monitored wherever they go. When enough people have these devices attached, there will be no more privacy, and the government (or whoever) will have achieved the perfect surveillance state, one that allows them to spy on everyone, detect any hint of insurrection, and crush any opposition before it even starts. These trackers can be administered in many ways (including vaccines). It's a dystopian nightmare, and it's coming your way very soon, all thanks to the RFID chip.

Except, not really. The components of this wireless system are the tags themselves and readers. Tags can do nothing on their own; they simply contain encoded information about the thing they are attached to. They are not cameras, or beacons, or radio transmitters, or anything else. In order to function, they need readers that can locate them. And these readers don't just track the tags in some sort of super science-fiction, almost magical, way. Readers need antennae to be able to do this.

Tags can be picked up on different frequencies, depending on the type of tag. So, only a reader designed to track the particular type of tag is going to be able to do it. This means that if there is no reader in range, that tracked item will not be, well, trackable. It might simply disappear—not very helpful for a universal surveillance system. Further, it's been shown that certain outside elements, like water, can interfere with tracking accuracy. Now, how much water does a human body have? About 70 percent, so in order to track a person, special modifications have to be made, and again, there is no guarantee that they will always work.

In order to track a person effectively, there would have to be thousands (if not more) readers in their general area in order not to lose them. And if they traveled too far away, they'd be lost anyway. It would be ridiculously complicated to set up a system that could track even one person, let alone millions, everywhere they went, twenty-four hours a day.

Conspiracy theorists will scoff at this dismissal, and say that such technology either already exists, or is being developed and will be ready soon. And we're back to the burden-of-proof issue again. The idea of evil, universal surveillance makes for a good story, but the science doesn't back it up.

GOVERNMENT TECHNOLOGY SUPPRESSION

ONE OF THE MORE POPULAR BELIEFS in conspiracy circles is that amazing, life-changing technologies already exist, but that various entities, such as the government or corporations, are working constantly to keep them hidden and suppressed, because they don't want all the benefits these new inventions and ideas could bring. If it's corporations, it's because they are trying to prevent being put out of business by newer tech that makes what they control obsolete. Here is a short list of some of the most popular theories about the tech that's supposedly being hidden and kept from us:

Electric cars were better than gas-powered ones, right from the beginning. These days, electric cars and hybrids are all the rage, and most major automobile manufacturers are eager to get in on the craze and make their own. However, one theory says that these cars were actually already very efficient 100 years ago, but that oil companies conspired to keep them off the roads and out of consumers' hands. But these early designs were not efficient and couldn't travel long distances, plus they were more expensive. People wanted what worked at that moment and what let them travel farther, so gas engines won out.

Electric lightbulbs were already far more efficient in the 1920s, but the electricity industry made them inefficient to increase sales. The idea is that a typical 1920s lightbulb could burn for up to 150,000 hours (about seventeen years!), but lightbulbs were degraded so that they would only work for about 1,000 hours at most. But the fact is that longer-burning bulbs actually use up more electricity and end up costing the consumer more over time, so even if they could work for seventeen years, they would be more expensive in the long run.

There are various sources of free energy that would do away with all the costs of creating it, but industries and the government have hidden them. This is probably the most popular of the suppressed technology theories. Whether it's perpetual-motion machines, cold fusion, power from the atmosphere, or a half dozen other ideas, there is a strong belief that "free energy" has been achieved, but again, oil and nuclear power companies don't want to be put out of business, so they have suppressed these ideas, bought up the patents, and so on. The reality is that energy is not a "something for nothing" exchange; that's just the basic laws of physics. You don't get energy out of something without putting energy into it. Fusion certainly exists; it's what the sun and all stars do. But it's very tricky to make it work here on Earth, and so-called "cold fusion" has been studied and found to be very unlikely. Sadly, free energy isn't really a thing, though new developments in technology will certainly make our energy more efficient as time goes on.

It turns out that suppressing certain technologies would probably cost a whole lot more than just letting them happen and taking advantage of them (e.g., electric cars) when the time is right.

MEDICAL CURE SUPPRESSION

FOR ALL THE ADVANCES in medical science in the last fifty years, there are some things that remain frustratingly out of reach: a definitive cure for cancer, for example, or a true treatment for AIDS. Even the common cold keeps coming around every year to annoy us. But for some conspiracy theorists, cures for most ills already exist, but the powers that be and the forces of economic and political pressure have conspired to keep them a secret. The idea is that Big Pharma has a vested interest in keeping people sick. Sick is good for business, after all. So therefore, if a miracle cure is found, one or more drug companies (or other institutions) buy up the patents and bury them, so that such cures can never be given proper clinical trials, much less be released to the public. The idea is similar to technology suppression; those companies who want to keep making money off of old methods that aren't as effective have no incentive to develop new ones that would take a bite out of their profits.

In 2000, self-proclaimed expert Kevin Trudeau brought out a self-published book, *Natural Cures "They" Don't Want You to Know About*, which made the claim that natural or suppressed cures exist for almost every human ailment, from cancer to herpes, from AIDS to multiple sclerosis, from diabetes to depression. All of these afflictions, he claimed, were curable through a combination of natural remedies and lifestyle choices. But this information was being suppressed by the US government and the FDA.

This obviously controversial book was a hit with many, but it also brought down criticism and condemnation. The book didn't list the cures, of course; after buying it, you had to go to his website and purchase a membership to "unlock" that information, a classic bait-and-switch. Trudeau himself has been found guilty of fraud and theft, and has been fined multiple times. Of course, to his supporters, this is simply proof that the establishment is out to get him.

The fact is that scientific and medical research can proceed at a very slow pace. Some diseases are more easily cured than others. Cancer, for example, is not one disease, but many, and it has numerous causes, so it's highly unlikely that a single miracle cure will be found. Progress on an AIDS vaccine continues and is showing promise again. We only need to look at how quickly the COVID-19 vaccines were developed to see that, sometimes, medical research can be very fast, indeed (more on COVID and its conspiracy theories later in this chapter).

And, yes, it's true: not every pharmaceutical company is always ethical. There have been many cases of one or another downplaying the negative side effects of their drugs, or engaging in some unethical behavior. But to suppose that there is a secret cabal controlling the world's access to medical cures is unlikely, to say the least. If a promising cure for something was found, it's more likely that money-hungry companies would rush to try to find their own version (or even steal the research) as soon as possible, to get it out to the market and make a fortune. In this case, greed is probably one of the best arguments against a company hoarding miracle cures.

AIDS WAS MADE IN A LABORATORY

AIDS SWEPT THROUGH THE WORLD beginning in the early 1980s, changing cultural and personal practices for good. It was a mysterious disease that was difficult to identify at first. When it was finally identified as being caused by the HIV virus, it seemed like there were some answers at last, and hope for a cure. Sadly, that wasn't to be the case,

though for many, HIV is now more of a chronic condition that can be managed, rather than a death sentence. The lack of a cure has led some people to believe that this insidious disease is too complex to have occurred naturally, and that it was probably manufactured, perhaps as a bioweapon, in a laboratory.

Jakob Segal, a biology professor at Humboldt University in East Germany (in the 1980s), proposed that HIV had been created by the US government in a military laboratory at Fort Detrick in Maryland. Researchers had spliced together two different viruses, creating a new hybrid virus in 1977 or 1978. The virus was tested on inmates at a nearby prison, who volunteered for the trial in exchange for early release. This, according to Segal, was how AIDS made it into the general population in the late 1970s and early 1980s.

It was quite an astonishing and damning theory. The problem with it is that it was nothing more than Soviet propaganda. The KGB created a disinformation campaign called "Operation DENVER" (at first thought to be called "Operation INFEKTION") that specifically blamed the United States for trying to manufacture an illegal bioweapon, and accidentally releasing it on the world as AIDS. It seems that when Segal wrote up a report about this, he was guessing, rather than basing his assertions on direct evidence. But it was enough to get the idea out there and to make some people really think about it. The report was denounced by mainstream scientists around the world, and was soon discarded as nonsense.

HIV has since been proven to have first appeared in humans as early as 1959 (in a blood sample), and it's thought that transmissions of a similar type of virus in African chimpanzees occurred as early as the 1920s. The killing of chimps and eating them as bushmeat might have contributed to the cross-species transmission. So, AIDS is definitely not a laboratory-made virus.

But that hasn't stopped believers from hanging on to some version of the theory. In the early 1990s, as many as 15 percent of the US population believed that the virus was created, and even in the mid-2000s, belief in a bioweapon made by the military or CIA was still strong in some groups, especially among African Americans. These beliefs probably grew up independently of any KGB propaganda, and show that when we are confronted with something that we can't control, it's very easy to slip into believing conspiracy theories to explain it.

COVID-19 CONSPIRACIES

COVID-19 SWEPT ACROSS THE WORLD beginning in 2020, a pandemic unlike anything since the influenza pandemic of 1918. As of late 2021, it has infected over 200 million people and killed over five million. It has made mask-wearing a common practice, and people all over the world have tried to isolate themselves and practice social distancing to slow its spread. But, of course, it has also been politicized, and this has led to fierce arguments over what to do about it. Some people think there is more to the story than it just being an animal disease that jumped to humans. Here are some of the most common conspiracy theories:

It was created in a lab. Research shows that this particular virus, like AIDS and some others, originated in animals but made the jump to humans, in this case in the Wuhan region of China. But some people insist that it was actually developed as a biological weapon by the Chinese government, and that it was released, whether accidentally or on purpose. Government officials hid this from the population and manufactured the story that it was naturally occurring. Several studies have debunked this claim.

It was created to cull the population. Whether by the Chinese, or by other shadowy organizations and government representatives, COVID was actually created for the purpose of wiping out large portions of the global population. Population control has long been a goal of some of these mystery groups, so the theory goes, and this is yet another example of what they will do. Obviously, there is no way to prove this theory.

It's no worse than the flu. This theory suggests that COVID is basically harmless, no worse than the flu, and that the entire exercise has been to bring people under control and make them live in fear. The idea is that people will be easier to manipulate if they fear for their lives and stay home. The COVID death rates as opposed to flu deaths debunk this theory.

The vaccine is intended to track people. Bill Gates and his vaccine initiatives have come under fire from some conspiracy theorists in the past, and they see the worldwide COVID vaccination drive as his (and others') attempt to install tracking devices in everyone who receives the shots. Governments and secretive groups will then be able to monitor them, spy on them, and crack down on dissent much more easily. It's a "mark of the beast," according to the more religiously paranoid. See the entry on RFID earlier in the chapter for why this theory is nonsense.

It's caused by 5G. COVID isn't really a disease at all, according to this theory. It's actually a response to the poison being put out by 5G technology, the fifth-generation mobile network wireless technology meant to speed up and improve internet and phone communications

worldwide. Some people maintain that the wireless frequencies are disrupting the body's ability to function, and causing all sorts of mysterious illnesses. What the establishment is calling an infectious disease is actually a response to the damaging 5G waves all around us. No one wants to admit that 5G has gone too far, so they invented a fake disease to hide that fact. This idea has also been debunked numerous times; data about COVID as an infectious disease is easily available.

HAARP

"HAARP" IS NOT A MISSPELLING; it's an acronym for High-frequency Active Auroral Research Program, which was based at a US government facility in Alaska and run by the US Air Force. The facility was made up of 180 identical antennae, spread out across forty acres of land. It was created to study the weather and how certain particles act in the ionosphere. This is the part of the atmosphere that helps radio transmissions go from one place to another. The facility studied these to better understand the damaging effects of solar flares (which often mean trouble for electronic devices and radio transmissions). The program was shut down in 2014.

But, of course, there was much more to HAARP than that! The facility was off-limits to the general public, and only people with special clearances were allowed in. And that must mean they had something to hide, right?

So, what was the HAARP facility really doing? There are many conspiracy theories: weather control, creating earthquakes, and even mind control. These experiments were being done so the military could gain new advantages over America's enemies. Imagine being able to control earthquakes in an enemy-occupied territory, or being able to send a massive thunderstorm over an approaching enemy army. Maybe a hurricane could be directed at the coastline of a hostile nation. We could completely dominate them in no time! And mind control . . . if we could do that, we could simply make enemy combatants throw down their weapons and surrender! Yep, supposedly all of this was going on at the HAARP facility, and probably a whole lot more.

Some people have gone so far as to speculate that climate change was caused by various HAARP experiments. Since HAARP was studying the ionosphere by using those antennae to heat up small portions of it, it was obviously doing something to weather patterns as well, and now we're in the situation that we're in. Is global warming the result of some mad scientist's experiments gone terribly wrong, all under the direction of the Air Force?

It makes for a great conspiracy theory, but there's no evidence that anything like that ever happened. Legitimate climate scientists have noted that the total amount of energy that HAARP generated was way less than even a single flash of lightning. There are thousands of lightning flashes around the world every day, and those have nothing to do with climate change. And how would focusing on the ionosphere cause earthquakes? The conspiracy theorists' answer is, of course, they were doing earthquake experiments deep in an underground portion of the site. And mind control? How would that work on people from such a remote location? Well, again, maybe they had secret facilities under-ground, away from prying eyes and out in the wilderness. In any case, HAARP ended in 2014. Or . . . did it?

A SECRET MOON MISSION

ACCORDING TO "OFFICIAL" HISTORY and statements, the NASA Apollo moon missions ended in 1972 with Apollo 17. Representatives at NASA have stated that the reason was not some big secret; it was simply a matter of money. Sending men to the moon cost an "astronomical" amount in those days, and NASA felt that it had learned all it needed to from the moon for the time being. So, while there were Apollo 18,

19, and 20 missions initially planned, they were scrapped. NASA chose instead to focus on its Skylab program in 1973 and 1974, and shift over to working on Earth-orbiting missions for astronauts.

That seems reasonable and logical, but according to some, it's simply not true. There was something up there, they say, and NASA wanted to get a better look in secret, especially before the Soviet Union could get to it. But what was so important that NASA had to go back in secret to look at it? In most cases, conspiracy theorists will say that it was evidence of alien life—perhaps a monument (think *2001: A Space Odyssey*), the ruins of a base, or some starship debris—or that the moon itself is a giant spaceship, etc. So NASA pretended to end the missions, but launched at least one more in secret to get the answers it wanted. And, of course, the agency and the government immediately covered up their findings.

The hype around this idea was enhanced in 2011, when a fake documentary movie, *Apollo 18*, was released. This was a science fiction–horror film that claimed to use "found footage" of a secret mission in 1974 that went horribly wrong. The film has been called "*The Blair Witch Project* in space." In this story, the astronauts are told that they are going on a secret mission to the moon, which will be disguised as a satellite launch. Once on the moon, they find a dead Russian cosmonaut, meaning that the Soviets were already there in secret too. Things go from bad to worse as they realize that they are not alone and that something lives on the moon: rocky, spiderlike creatures that don't appreciate their home being invaded.

It's all great fun, but there's nothing true about it. While the film uses actual NASA footage of other moon orbits and landings, it's just a fake documentary that's meant to look real. Still, a number of people believed it was a true story, and the movie only made the decades-long whispers about secret NASA missions more popular.

So, was there ever a secret moon mission, or several of them? And if so, what did they find? Well, it's highly unlikely. A former NASA engineer named John Schuessler commented that it would simply have been impossible for a mission that large and expensive to have been kept secret. There was no time of day that it could have been done; someone

would have noticed a launch. And while Schuessler has actually studied UFOs seriously, he says that not only was there no way that this secret mission could have happened, there also is absolutely no evidence of alien life (or its remains) on the moon.

Of course, that's what they want you to think. . . .

CERN LARGE HADRON COLLIDER

THE PARTICLE COLLIDER IN SWITZERLAND has been the subject of conspiracy theories since well before it was even built. It has been suspected of everything from contacting parallel universes to creating mini black holes that could accidentally wipe out everything. One of the more interesting conspiracy theories associated with CERN is that we ceased to exist a few years ago, only we don't know it yet. Huh?

According to some, the end of the world actually did happen back in 2012, a doomsday year that lots of people thought would signal the end of the world. Remember all the stuff about December 21, 2012? Yeah, that really happened just as the Mayan calendar predicted it would, only we didn't notice.

Okay, if you're lost, you're not alone. This story is more than a little bit weird, but there are some conspiracy theorists who really do seem to think such a wacky scenario is true. So what happened? There was an accident at the CERN collider, a bad one. While it was going about its usual search for subatomic particles, such as the famed Higgs boson "God particle," it did something else scientists didn't intend.

Researchers at CERN accidentally created a mini black hole, small but powerful enough to swallow the entire Earth. That should have been the end of it, but scientists had access to secret technology, known only to a few (maybe from aliens, maybe from another dimension), that was able to make perfect copies of all of us and the Earth and save everything as a simulation. People didn't even notice what happened. They simply were obliterated one day, but instantly recreated as copies of themselves, completely unaware that anything had happened. Advanced science was able to recreate our existence and we continue on now, perfect copies of what the black hole destroyed.

If you're thinking this sounds pretty ridiculous, you're right. As usual, there is no evidence at all for these theories, or any explanation about how such a simulation could be built, set up, and running in the background while a black hole was devouring us. And if the black hole devoured everything, where would the source of this simulation be now? In another dimension? In a pocket dimension? Inside the black hole itself? Again, nobody knows, and explanations are either missing or even crazier than the theory itself.

It's pretty fair to say that there is a huge chance the Earth didn't get devoured in 2012, and we're not all living in some scientists' idea of a fancy video game. Even if one accepts the idea that we might be actually living in a simulation, this doesn't seem like a very possible explanation for how we got into it!

THE MOON LANDINGS WERE FAKED

ONE OF THE ALL-TIME GRANDDADDY CLASSICS of conspiracy theories is that the United States never went to the moon, not even once. The whole program was a fake to increase America's standing in the world in opposition to the Soviets. The government hid everything from the public, and to this day, most people believe we went to the moon. The scenes allegedly on the moon were shot on a film studio soundstage, under great security and secrecy. Some even claim that legendary director Stanley Kubrick directed the sequences to ensure that they looked convincing. People who believe this theory offer up a number of reasons as to why they think it's true, but these have all been addressed and debunked, not only by NASA, but by countless independent scientists and astronomers as well. Still, here is a sampling of them:

Stars are not visible in the sky. This is one of the most common accusations: the fact that pictures show only an all-black background "proves" that the "moon" was actually just a soundstage. But it doesn't. The stars are washed out because of the light of the sun, just as they are on Earth during daytime. The sky is black because space is black, and there is no atmosphere on the moon to change that color. Also, the astronauts used quick exposures on their cameras, so the stars simply wouldn't show up.

The American flag is "flapping." It looks as if the flag planted on the moon is blowing in the wind. But without an atmosphere, it shouldn't be moving at all. So, clearly, it was filmed on Earth. Except that this flag is special. If it were an ordinary cloth flag, it would hang just as a flag does on Earth on a nonwindy day. This one was fitted with a horizontal rod to hold it out, and, when unfurled, it looked like it was flapping. That's all.

The shadows are wrong. Some claim that because you can see certain items in shadow, there must be another light source, i.e., stage lights. Otherwise, the shadowed areas would be black, since the sun is the only source of light. But there is another light source: the surface of the moon, which is white and reflective.

The astronauts wouldn't have left footprints. You need moisture, like mud, to leave footprints, right? Since the moon has none, there should be none. Well, that's not true. Fine particles can hold shapes; think of cornstarch. And since there is no weather on the moon, those footprints are still up there and will be for millions of years.

The radiation outside Earth's atmosphere is deadly. The theory is that the radiation in the Van Allen belt outside of the Earth would be too intense and would kill anyone who entered it, long before they were even able to set foot on the moon. But, again, this isn't true. The astronauts were not exposed long enough for the radiation to have a damaging effect.

It's worth noting that the Soviets had a vested interest in debunking the American achievement. They would have been delighted to prove that the moon landings were a hoax, but they never did. They never even tried. And something like 400,000 people worked on the Apollo missions. That's a whole lot of people to expect to keep their mouths shut if it was all faked!

THE FLAT EARTH

THIS THEORY HAS ENJOYED a huge resurgence of popularity in recent years. Scientists and many others are shaking their heads in disbelief as the idea of a flat Earth, a relic of a long-ago age of superstition, is making a comeback with a lot of people who really should know better. For the record, Columbus and the other Renaissance explorers didn't "prove" that the Earth was round to skeptical Europeans; knowledge that the Earth was a globe had existed in various forms going back to Greek and Roman times, and probably much earlier.

A belief that was once part of the fringe has weirdly become almost mainstream. So why is this relic from the past popular again today, in spite of all the evidence that we live on a globe? Some of it has to do with a lack of good science education, of course, but often it's more to do with a belief that people can't trust anyone in authority anymore. While belief in a flat Earth skews a bit more to the right and to the deeply religious, theorists of all political stripes and beliefs have signed on to it. And one belief that seems to unite them is that the moon landings were a hoax. Oh, and that NASA (of course) is hiding the truth.

So, how do people envision a flat Earth? Usually, it's seen as a disc, with the North Pole at the center, around which the continents swirl. What we call the continent of Antarctica is actually an ice barrier at the edge that prevents ocean water from spilling over the edge and being lost to space. The sun circles the Earth, which creates day and night, while the moon is much smaller than claimed and much closer to the flat Earth around which it orbits. Some believe in an "anti-moon" which we never see. Needless to say, Flat Earthers also reject the theory of gravity as

Most people would consider these ideas absurd, so how do believers justify them? They've come up with various calculations and assertions to prove their case, such as how the curved horizon is not visible at great heights (actually, it is). One believer even used a level on an airplane, which he says stayed level the entire time, instead of adjusting for a supposed curvature, which proved to him that the Earth is flat. Scientists have tended to roll their eyes and ignore these ill-informed expressions of so-called scientific testing, but many are rightly concerned about what this says about the greater population. One study showed that 84 percent of younger Americans surveyed believed in a round Earth; that's a whole lot of others who are at least a little bit unsure, even if only 2 to 4 percent of them are convinced that the Earth is flat.

A renewed commitment to better science education is one way to combat this silly belief, but also working to restore people's belief in science and to not accept every conspiracy theory that comes along would be a great help!

WE'RE LIVING IN A SIMULATION

WHILE THE WORLD AROUND US seems pretty obviously solid—something we can see, touch, smell, hear, and taste—there are some people who believe that it's all fake, basically a computer simulation. Nothing is really real; it's only how our brains are interacting with a very complex program. Of course, this immediately brings to mind the *Matrix* films, and the first thought you might have is that the idea is just science fiction. But interestingly, a lot of very intelligent people seem to think that it could at least be possible. The idea is pretty simple: since we can make imaginary worlds, computer games, and simulations, what are the chances that our own world, our own universe, is itself made up by someone else?

It has to do with the idea of "base" reality. In other words, is our reality the first or "base" reality, and all of our games and simulations are our

own creations, or are we ourselves creations for another base reality that we don't know about? Those who believe in this conspiracy theory say that we are actually a simulation too, and that either no one really knows the truth, or only a small number of people have figured it out and are keeping it secret, again rather like the *Matrix* movies.

So, are we all simulations? Is this the greatest secret and conspiracy theory of all? How would we know? It might disturb you, but there really is no way to know for sure if we are living in the base reality or not. What kind of test would we use to figure it out? Whoever was controlling our simulation could just program something new to change the outcome, and keep the simulation hidden from us. Now, in science, if a question like this can't even be tested, then it is usually considered something not worth checking into, because there is no way to prove it one way or another.

The philosopher Bertrand Russell came up with an idea that explains this. If someone says that there is a small teapot orbiting the sun out between Earth and Mars, it's probably not true, but there is no way to absolutely prove that it's false. Still, the person who says so has to prove it somehow, and, of course, they can't. So, if we live in a simulation, the person who says we do has to prove it somehow.

That would seem to be the end of the argument, but some very smart mathematicians and other folks have decided to try to calculate the odds anyway, and, surprisingly, they say that even without conclusive proof, the chances that we do live in some kind of simulation could be as high as fifty-fifty! Of course, we have no way of knowing if we are a simulation for a base reality, or if we are several simulations away from that base reality. It's enough to make your head hurt! And here's an even more uncomfortable thought: What if we are living in a simulation and whoever created it just decides one day to turn it off?

THE MOON IS ARTIFICIAL

ONE OF THE GRANDER CONSPIRACY THEORIES out there is that the moon is not a natural satellite that formed billions of years ago, but is, in fact, artificial, made by unknown alien beings for unknown purposes. Now, the conventional thought about the moon is that it was made when a Mars-sized object collided with the proto-Earth around fifty million years after the solar system formed, releasing huge amounts of matter that eventually formed into our rather large-sized moon that has orbited our planet ever since. The exact way that the moon came into being is unknown, but this explanation best fits the evidence.

But the standard scientific explanation doesn't sit too well with some people, who think there are some curious features about the satellite that make it unlikely to be natural. In 1970, Michael Vasin and Alexander Shcherbakov, two members of the Soviet Academy of Sciences, published an article in which they speculated that the moon was hollow and was, in fact, an ancient spaceship of some kind. Of course, they didn't publish this in a scientific journal, but rather in *Sputnik*, which was kind of a Soviet *Reader's Digest*.

They wrote:

> The Moon is an artificial Earth satellite put into orbit around the Earth by some intelligent beings unknown to ourselves. We refuse to engage in speculation about who exactly staged this unique experiment, which only a highly developed civilization was capable of.

> If you are going to launch an artificial sputnik, then it is advisable to make it hollow. At the same time it would be naive to imagine that anyone capable of such a tremendous space project would be satisfied simply with some kind of giant empty trunk hurled into a near-Earth trajectory.

> It is more likely that what we have here is a very ancient spaceship, the interior of which was filled with fuel for the engines, materials

and appliances for repair work, navigation, instruments, observation equipment and all manner of machinery. . . . In other words, everything necessary to enable this "caravel of the Universe" to serve as a kind of Noah's Ark of intelligence, perhaps even as the home of a whole civilization envisaging a prolonged (thousands of millions of years) existence and long wanderings through space (thousands of millions of miles).

As evidence, they pointed out that it was curious that the moon's craters, even when very wide, were not as deep as they should be, given the size of the impacts. They theorized that this was because, under the rocky surface, there is a hard metal interior: the hull of the spaceship. As for why the moon is here, they were not sure, but speculated that its advanced inhabitants might have long since died, leaving the ship to orbit the Earth. Of course, no one took this theory seriously, especially the Soviet government, but it has found devotees over the years, and many people (once again!) assume that NASA knows the truth and is covering it up. The Apollo astronauts were said to have claimed that the moon rang like a bell, which would prove it is hollow. In 2007, two authors, Christopher Knight and Alan Butler, wrote a book called *Who Built the Moon?* that explored the possibilities of the moon being artificial. While the book has its fans, scientists dismissed it as nonsense.

OTHER NASA CONSPIRACIES

IN ADDITION TO FAKING THE MOON LANDINGS, NASA is apparently going full-time on hoodwinking the general public with lies, cover-ups, and all-around sneakiness. It's a wonder its scientists have time to do any actual space missions! Since there are so many conspiracies to follow, here is a short list of some of the more popular ones that are always circulating online, which "prove" that NASA must spend most of its budget on hiding the truth from the people who pay its employees' salaries. But never fear! A group of intrepid conspiracy theorists have found those truths, and here they are!

NASA's elite are "Masonic Satanists." Or Illuminati members. Or part of the New World Order. Or something that controls what the agency says to the world, and makes it put out false information constantly. But NASA also includes deep meanings behind its space launches, which have Masonic or other symbolism. Even the dates and times of launches and landings, the turning on of cameras, the naming of missions . . . all of them have mystical symbolism known only to a hidden few. Except for those theorists who have figured them out, of course.

NASA hides proof of alien life. NASA already knows that aliens are here, and that they have been on the moon, Mars (see the next paragraph), and a good number of other planets and moons in our solar system. Artifacts, monuments, buildings, etc., are everywhere, but NASA has done a good job of keeping the whole business quiet, since the government (or whoever controls it) has told it to.

NASA knows the truth about Mars. There was once an advanced civilization on Mars, and NASA has evidence for it. A few of the bigger monuments that these aliens built, such as the giant face-like image on the surface that was discovered back in 1976, are objects the agency can't ignore, so it doctors photos of them now to make them look like natural rock formations. Whole websites are devoted to analyzing every photo NASA releases of Mars to look for evidence of tampering and to calculate shapes, sizes, and distances between geological formations on the surface in order to show signs of intelligent design.

NASA is hiding evidence of a doomsday asteroid. A massive asteroid called Apophis is on a collision course with Earth and will strike it in either 2029, or 2036, or 2068. It was discovered in 2004, and at first, astronomers were indeed concerned that it might pass close enough to Earth to hit the planet, but calculations have since set minds at ease; they've ruled out any chance of an impact for at least 100 years. Of course, that's what NASA and others want us to believe. We are actually on a collision course with this doomsday asteroid, and there's nothing we can do about it, or so the internet says.

NASA's whole purpose is a lie. NASA doesn't actually do much, apparently. It might have been created in an attempt to keep up with the

Soviets in the 1950s, to start a so-called "space race" to make it look like the United States was doing something about space exploration. It was an effort to save face with the international community, but in addition to faking the moon landings, most of its other projects are also fake. All those gorgeous photos of other planets, and even of the Earth itself, are fakes, because at this point, the government can't admit what it's been doing for over sixty years.

CHEMTRAILS

YOU'VE PROBABLY LOOKED UP to the sky and many times seen a stream of white vapor reaching across it, and sometimes more than one. You might even see several of them, crisscrossed and making Xs in the sky. These are the condensation trails of airlines and other aircraft, which are left behind as they fly through. They tend to disperse after a few minutes. They're known as "contrails," and you've seen them and probably taken little or no notice of them, because they're here one minute and gone the next. But for some conspiracy theorists, there is way more to the story, and it's decidedly unpleasant. To them, some of these lines might indeed be vapor trails, but at least some of them are serving a much more nefarious purpose.

Those who believe in the idea of these "chemtrails" say that they are different from normal contrail condensation, that they linger in the air longer, and that they are being used for reasons unknown to the general public. What reasons? Well, there are different theories. Here are few of the most popular:

Weather control: Some think that these chemicals might be sprayed into the upper atmosphere to help certain kinds of weather come about, such as in a drought-stricken area that needed more rain. But if this were true, why wouldn't it be used in such areas more often? Why do severe droughts continue? There is already a technology for "cloud seeding" that isn't secret, so what would be the point, unless it is to control the weather for offensive, even military purposes. . . .

Solar radiation control: With climate change being a great concern, some believe that these chemtrails are an attempt to spray tiny reflective particles into the air to act as a buffer against sunlight. The idea is that they would reflect light and heat back out into space, and thus help reduce global warming. But while this might seem like a noble idea, it's putting potentially dangerous materials into our atmosphere, and we don't yet know what the long-term effects will be.

Mind control: Some believe that the chemicals in these trails are intended to sink down to the surface and affect people's moods, making them easier to control. Believers see the rise in conditions like depression and anxiety as a possible proof that people's minds and emotions are secretly being tampered with.

Population control: Some believe that these chemicals are even more insidious, and are intended to poison people's bodies and reduce fertility. They point to falling fertility rates in the United States and elsewhere as proof of this belief. The point is to bring population numbers down without people knowing or consenting.

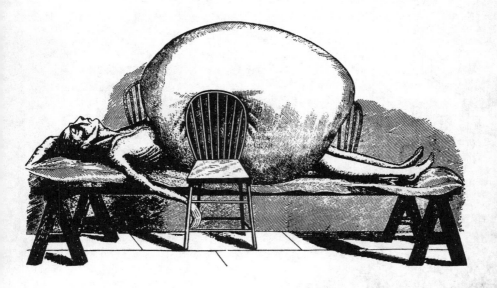

Biological and chemical warfare: Some believe that chemtrails are test runs for biological and chemical warfare delivery via planes. These could have a devastating effect on an enemy population, but smaller doses might be released over American civilians to see how well such toxic chemicals infiltrate the air and water in a given area. People are unknowing guinea pigs in a horrendous experiment.

Needless to say, the scientific community rejects all of these assertions, and there have been several studies conducted to show that there is no truth to them. But that doesn't deter believers, who point to occasional anomalies in the chemical content in soil and water as proof.

Is the government poisoning its people? Some definitely think so.

CLIMATE CHANGE DENIALISM

THERE IS A BROAD CONSENSUS among the world's climate and earth scientists that human activity is drastically changing the natural climate of the planet, causing it to warm at an abnormally high rate. Evidence shows that this change—also known as "global warming"—has been happening at consistent and predictable rates since the time of the Industrial Revolution. The burning of fossil fuels is pouring larger amounts of carbon dioxide—one of the "greenhouse gasses"—into the atmosphere, trapping a certain amount of heat from the sun. The planet Venus is an example of this effect taken to hellish extremes. Action must be taken to slow down the amount of this gas being put into our atmosphere, and to slow down warming. Otherwise, glaciers will continue to melt, oceans will continue to rise, and the melting of permafrost will release more greenhouse gasses and potentially dangerous pathogens into the world.

While the studies on climate change are many and extensive, there are still some who refuse to believe that it's happening, or at least deny that human behavior has anything to do with it. They insist there is a conspiracy to go along with this view, and that evidence pointing to the contrary is suppressed or just ignored. So, what do climate change denialists claim? Here are some of their accusations:

Limiting freedoms. By imposing strict new regulations on things such as car emissions, gasoline and oil, heating, and the use of solar power, governments worldwide can further restrict freedoms and make their citizens more compliant. By scaring people into believing that coastal cities might flood, they can herd them to other locations.

Establishing a world government. Once freedoms are limited, people will be more susceptible to a totalitarian/communist/world government takeover (take your pick). By keeping people in a state of fear, those pulling the strings can impose worldwide climate goals (such as those established in previous conferences), which will further remove each country's sovereignty, and force them to obey laws they didn't make.

Pushing for more green energy. Solar and other "green" technology companies are pushing the hoax because it will be increasingly profitable for them. Because oil companies would never promote climate change denial so that they could continue to make money, apparently.

Pushing for more nuclear power. The nuclear industry would like to build more power plants, and one way to do that is to get everyone to abandon fossil fuels, just like the green energy companies are allegedly doing.

A foreign plot. China or some other government created the climate change hoax to make the United States "less competitive," by handcuffing itself to unnecessary regulations. Former president Donald Trump and others have insisted this is true for many years.

Could any of these be true? Most sound pretty far-fetched, and the scientific evidence for human-caused climate change is compelling. But conspiracy theorists will probably continue to insist on the veracity of one or more of these ideas, even when they're up to their knees in rising ocean waters.

'T is onſ profyt

BIRDS AREN'T REAL

WHAT? At first, this idea seems to be so bizarre that no one could possibly take it seriously. How are birds not real? We literally see dozens, if not hundreds, of them every day, whether we live in cities or out in the middle of the country. Chirps, squawks, screeches, and twitters abound in the air at all times of the year, and our feathered friends are often delightful companions. Well, some say that, yes, there are things out there that look like birds, but they are not actually birds. Okay . . .

According to this theory, in the 1950s, the CIA wanted a new opportunity to spy on Americans. It was the height of the Cold War, and fears of communism abounded. So, it seemed wise to find out who among the public were communist sympathizers. They hatched a plan (see what we did there?) to kill some twelve billion birds and replace them with lifelike drones that would be able to monitor every neighborhood for suspicious activities without being detected themselves. In fact, when President Kennedy refused to go along with the plan, they had him assassinated. The fake birds were put in place. And they've been spying on us ever since, right under the nose of the American public.

Yes, this conspiracy theory is ridiculous. And the thing is, the person who created it knows that too! Peter McIndoe, a student at the University of Memphis in Tennessee, came up with the idea in early 2017. A video of him holding up signs proclaiming that birds are "fake" went viral and started a parody movement that soon sported its own histories and conspiracy theories about how these robot birds have been spying on Americans for decades. McIndoe was able to monetize his joke with merchandise proclaiming the "truth." Most people took it for what it was: a satirical spoof that was all in good fun.

But because no one can ever just enjoy anything anymore, and no matter what one says, there will always be someone taking it out of context, the "birds aren't real" movement has gained some genuine followers, often among those who are attracted to QAnon and similar fringe theories. For this small group of people, there might just be something to the whole idea. Many of them already believe that the government is spying on them anyway, so why not with robot birds? Thankfully, their numbers seem to be small, but really, the whole conspiracy theory is just bird-brained. . . .

CHAPTER 7
UFOS & OTHER UNKNOWNS

THERE COULD BE NO CONSPIRACY THEORY BOOK without at least a few entries on aliens! And while there are many good books on subjects like sightings and abductions, there are some fine examples of conspiratorial behavior to be found in UFO lore. The idea that the government secretly knows about alien life, and might even be in possession of technology and alien bodies (if not actual aliens themselves) is an essential part of the UFO phenomenon. Such knowledge is thought to be too dangerous to the population, and so is being kept secret.

This short chapter introduces some of the most famous examples of this theory, from Roswell to Hangar 18 to Area 51, all of which are said to be classic cases of very close encounters, so much so that certain authorities had to hide away what they'd found, even from most elected representatives. Of course, we could already be under the control of one group of aliens, and an ancient satellite might well be spying on us at this very moment. . . .

THE ROSWELL,
NEW MEXICO, INCIDENT

THE ALLEGED ALIEN SPACESHIP CRASH at Roswell is probably the most famous UFO event in history. It took place outside of a town called Roswell, New Mexico, in 1947, and captured the world's imagination. Despite officials denying that anything weird happened, there are many there who swore that it took place. If they're telling the truth, then it means that an alien craft crashed, and the government has not only the ship, but alien bodies too, and has been hiding this fact for more than seventy years.

Between July 2 and July 4, 1947, something odd definitely happened on a ranch. A craft of some kind crashed, and soon, government officials were on the scene, blocking off the area to the public. Barney Barnett, a government engineer, later said that he was at the ranch after the crash, and that he had seen alien bodies and some kind of crashed spacecraft.

Soon, rumors were getting out that the military had found something very strange. It was said that the material of the spaceship was very light in weight and had some writing on it, a bit like Egyptian hieroglyphics. But it was also very strong. It couldn't be bent, broken, or even burned. Some of it was only as thick as aluminum foil, but tests found that it could stop bullets. The alien bodies were reported to be small and hairless, with large heads and eyes. It was alleged that one alien had survived and was brought to a top-secret military base.

This was an incredible story, but it was about to get even weirder. An official report confirmed that an alien ship had crashed and alien bodies had been recovered! It was an amazing admission, but, of course, it didn't last. Not even a day later, another report said that the debris actually came from a new kind of weather balloon. Some even said that the "bodies" were actually crash-test dummies, like the kind used in cars. That's why they were hairless and odd looking.

Naturally, a lot of people didn't believe this backtracking and accused the government of trying to cover up what might be one of the most important events in world history. UFO skeptics went with the balloon

explanation, while believers insisted that the government was clearly lying. But why would they lie? Because if the story were true, it would be proof of an alien species with superior technology, a technology that we might not be able to defend against if they turned out to be hostile. To prevent a public panic, the theory goes, the government lied about it and secretly studied the debris and the alien bodies. Skeptics countered that the weather balloon might also be used for spying, so they might want to keep it secret.

To this day, no one knows for sure what happened, but a few high-ranking, retired military officials have come forward over the years to report that they believe that it was an alien ship. One of them even claimed that everyone from President Truman on down in rank knew that the ship was "not of this earth." Did an alien ship crash in the New Mexico desert? Is the government hiding proof of it? Have there been other alien encounters? Time might yet tell. . . .

AREA 51

IN THE DESERT OF NEVADA (northwest of Las Vegas), there is a region that is fenced off and not open to the public. Warning signs everywhere say that it is the property of the US government. You're not allowed in and cannot take photographs. If you go in anyway, you'll probably be arrested, and possibly charged with some crime. The signs even warn that the government has the authority to shoot anyone caught out there! Of course, this doesn't stop many curious people from visiting, often sneaking as close to the fence as they can late at night, just to try to get a look at what might be there. But why do they do it? Why take the risk? Because according to conspiracy theorists, Area 51 contains secret information about UFOs and aliens, and has at least one alien spacecraft. Scientists there are studying alien technology and might have alien bodies, or possibly living alien prisoners inside!

One of the most famous locations in all of UFO lore, Area 51 is definitely a real place, even though the government only admitted this in 2013. Officials say that they conduct tests of new and experimental aircraft there, which makes sense. The work is classified as top secret, which means that the public isn't allowed to know anything about it. For conspiracy theorists, this secret site is a perfect place for the testing of captured alien artifacts and spaceships, and this is the real reason that the government is so secretive.

Some people believe that debris from the Roswell crash was taken there to study, to see if the technology could be reverse engineered and used in our own fighter jets. Others will tell you that experiments in time travel, teleportation, and weather control happen there, or that captive aliens may be held prisoner deep in underground structures.

In 1989, a man named Bob Lazar claimed that he had worked with alien technology, mainly on the spacecraft that was held in Area 51. Soon after, a UFO documentary interviewed a man who claimed that he was an engineer who had worked on a flying disc simulator at Area 51 to train pilots, one that was based on the alien ship at the base. He also said that he worked with an alien nicknamed "J-Rod," who helped him to understand the advanced technology.

These are bold claims that can't be proven or disproven. There is no doubt that Area 51 is one of the most secret and guarded places in the world. Believe it or not, for a while, even satellites were not allowed to photograph it from orbit, and planes were not allowed to fly over it. What is so amazing out there that it needs to be kept so secret? Is it really just advanced jets and other experimental aircraft? Or is there something incredible hidden there that the government doesn't want the rest of the world to know about?

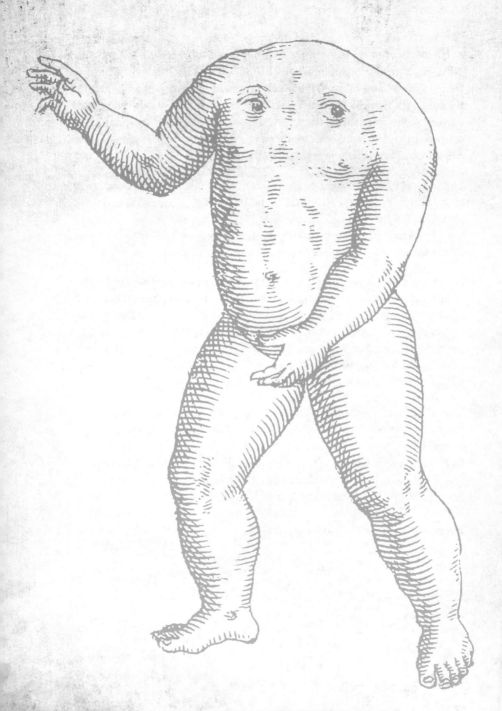

THE BIG BOOK OF CONSPIRACY THEORIES

HANGAR 18

DEPENDING ON WHO YOU BELIEVE, the Wright-Patterson Air Force Base outside of Dayton, Ohio, might have something truly amazing hidden away inside of it. Wright-Patterson is rumored to be similar to Area 51, in that some very strange and otherworldly things might be going on there. It's thought by some conspiracy theorists that one building on the site, known as Hangar 18, contains secret information about alien life and technology. Like Area 51, it allegedly holds alien spacecraft and alien bodies. In fact, samples of both were taken here from the Roswell crash, believers say, and other specimens have shown up there over the years. All of this is said to be hidden in a high-security, top-secret place in Hangar 18 known as the Blue Room.

A former military pilot, Oliver Henderson, is said to have told his wife that he flew some of the material from Roswell, including spaceship debris and alien bodies, to Wright-Patterson in the days after the July 1947 crash. The children of another pilot, Marion Magruder, said that he told them he had seen a living alien at the base, one who died later due to the experiments conducted on it. Magruder was apparently angry about this.

No less than Senator Barry Goldwater of Arizona, the Republican nominee for president in 1964, became interested in these accounts. Goldwater was convinced that there was something to the whole story, and he requested access to the Blue Room to see for himself. Air Force General Curtis LeMay denied his request, telling him, "Not only can't you get into it, but don't you ever mention it to me again." Well, that was quite a defensive order! Goldwater went public about that denial in 1988. For many people, this definitely meant that something strange was happening.

In the 1970s, a UFO researcher named Robert Spencer Carr wrote in a book that a high-ranking military officer told him that Wright-Patterson was holding at least twelve alien bodies, and two saucer-shaped alien craft. But Carr seemed to have a reputation for inventing things to make his claims sound better, so he is probably not a reliable source.

The Air Force has never officially confirmed or denied any of these claims, but in January 1985, it issued an official statement about the base:

"Periodically, it is erroneously stated that the remains of extraterrestrial visitors are or have been stored at Wright-Patterson Air Force Base. There are not now, nor have there ever been, any extraterrestrial visitors or equipment on Wright-Patterson Air Force Base."

Of course, that might just be what they want you to believe. . . .

REPTILIAN OVERLORDS

WITH EVERYTHING THAT GOES WRONG in the world on an almost daily basis, there is a never-ending quest to find explanations for it all. As we saw in the Secret Societies chapter, many people believe that small, secretive groups of the very wealthy hold immense power and can manipulate the world behind the scenes, according to their whims. But the reptilian theory goes one step further and says that our slavers are not just the very wealthy, they are an elite group of interdimensional, shape-shifting lizards who hold this world in their grip!

There are many different versions of this conspiracy theory, but it has been laid out in most detail by British author David Icke, a former football (soccer) player and sports broadcaster. Icke's biography is rather long and complicated, but suffice to say that he had to abandon football due to issues with arthritis, and he worked for a time in broadcasting before beginning his own personal spiritual journey in the 1980s. After several encounters with teachers, healers, psychics, and others, he became convinced that he was a "Son of the Godhead" and had been sent to deliver important messages to the world. If this sounds like the beginnings of a new cult, it does, but the path that Icke chose instead was different and even stranger.

There has long been a portion of UFO studies that claims some of the aliens that people have seen resemble bipedal reptiles, and that they are usually much less calm and kind than the classic "greys." Icke developed his own version of the reptilians and laid it out in his 1994 book, *The*

Rebellion. In this book, Icke claims that a secret group of interdimensional beings, the so-called reptilians, are secretly controlling the Earth. Known as either the Archons or the Anunnaki, they are able to shape-shift and assume human form, which allows them to pass unnoticed to most. Archons were false gods in early Christian Gnostic belief, while the Anunnaki are referred to as gods in ancient Mesopotamian writings. For Icke, these were real beings, not myths, and were actually the reptilians.

Known as the "Babylonian Brotherhood," a group of reptilian-human hybrids have insinuated themselves into the corridors of power, and pose as world leaders. They actively try to keep humanity in a state of fear and anger by stirring up wars, hatred, greed, other conflicts, environmental problems, political instability, and so on. By doing this, they can literally feed off of the negative energy that humans give off in response to events around them. Their goal is ultimately a world fascist state under their control. The only way for humanity to defeat them is to wake up to what they are doing and embrace universal love, to drain them of their power.

The Brotherhood consists of every American president, quite a few other world leaders, the British royal family, wealthy families like the Rockefellers and Rothschilds, and various others in positions of power. They are all part of this hybrid species and can transform back and forth between human and reptilian at will. The change, Icke says, often can be detected in their eyes. Icke has been accused of anti-Semitism, as he believes *The Protocols of the Elders of Zion* (see the Historical Conspiracies chapter) is authentic, though it doesn't represent the Jews as a whole, merely a small number. Icke has embraced several other conspiracy theories (most recently, 5G causing COVID), and while the majority view him as something of a crackpot, he still has his devoted followers, even though he's never offered a shred of actual proof for his wild claims.

THE BLACK KNIGHT SATELLITE

RIGHT NOW, there are countless satellites, as well as plenty of junk, orbiting the Earth. We've sent so many objects up into orbit over the last sixty years that it's getting kind of crowded up there! But what if one of the things orbiting the planet was not something that we put there? What if it came from somewhere else? Enter: the Black Knight Satellite!

Believers in this conspiracy theory say that the BKS is an alien probe or satellite that has been making a polar orbit of the Earth for the last 13,000 years. It was sent by an unknown alien civilization, perhaps to observe primitive people and watch how humanity has developed over that long time. And according to some, it might still be watching us.

Where did it come from? Who sent it? No one knows, of course, and there are probably dozens of guesses and stories about those questions. But believers will tell you that it is definitely still there. NASA knows about it, but is covering it up, precisely because we have no idea who sent it and why. NASA and those at the top levels of government are trying to avoid a public panic, which would happen if people understood that aliens are out there, and there's nothing we can do about them. Worse, they're spying on us, and we don't know why!

Even more amazing, believers say that there is proof, not only from history, but in a photograph. In 1899, inventor Nikola Tesla conducted some experiments with radio waves and received back a series of mysterious sounds or signals, which he believed had been sent from another planet. Of course, no one really believed him at the time, but supporters of the BKS theory will tell you that he was picking up signals from the alien satellite. Astronomers now think that if Tesla did indeed detect something, it was probably from a pulsar, a distant magnetic rotating star that emits electromagnetic radiation.

More recently, BKS believers say, a photo from a space shuttle mission in 1998 captured the mysterious object on film. It is indeed something oddly shaped and black in color, which seems to be orbiting the Earth. NASA says that this was nothing more than a bit of space debris—likely a blanket that acts as a heat shield—and that it entered the atmosphere a few days after that photo was taken and burned up. The crew aboard the International Space Station confirmed that they lost one of their thermal coverings, and that this was probably what the shuttle crew saw as it floated away. But those who doubt this explanation have gone to great lengths to enhance the image and try to point out what seem like weird features, shapes, and other items that could be signs of alien technology, something completely beyond us.

Is an alien probe spying on us? Possibly, but it probably isn't the Black Knight Satellite, or the thermal blanket in the photo, drifting toward its doom.

CHAPTER 8
CELEBRITY & CULTURAL CONSPIRACIES

PEOPLE LOVE CELEBRITIES, if tabloids and entertainment magazines are anything to go by. Fans want to know the intimate details of the lives of the rich and famous, probably so that they can escape into the world of their heroes for a little while. Or maybe it's so they can see that even with money and fame, life isn't always that much better. Indeed, when something bad happens to a celebrity, it can lead to strong reactions from that person's fans. A death or disappearance is almost guaranteed to have some people theorizing that maybe there was more to the story. It helps them make sense of tragedy.

This final chapter looks at some of the amazing conspiracy theories about celebrities and pop culture, covering everything from suicides that might have been murders to hidden satanic messages in music, to the idea that some famous people are hiding some very dark secrets about themselves. It's probably unavoidable that if someone is well-known and loved for something, people will begin to make up wild stories about them, whether they are alive or dead. This chapter includes some of the best of those stories, from the possible to the truly bizarre.

THE DEATH OF MARILYN MONROE

ACTRESS MARILYN MONROE was found dead in her home in Los Angeles on August 5, 1962. The official investigation said that it had been a suicide, by an overdose of barbiturates. She had been a popular actress and sex symbol since the 1950s, but she was struggling with depression and addiction. Her previous film had been a box-office disappointment, and she had been fired from her most recent film, *Something's Got to Give* (which was never completed in that form) in June 1962. So it was understandable that she would be in a terrible state, and potentially suicidal. She had attempted suicide in the past, but had called for help and been rescued. Given the large number of drugs in her system and that she was locked in her bedroom, it seemed the obvious conclusion.

But not everyone was satisfied with this. It wasn't long before various conspiracy theories started floating around. Eventually, many books would be written about them, and what might have happened if she didn't kill herself. Here are a few of the most popular alternate theories about her fate on that night. Most of them have to do with her association with the Kennedy family.

She was killed on the orders of Robert Kennedy. Robert, the president's younger brother, was allegedly having an affair with her. Obviously, the affair would hurt his career prospects, and she threatened to expose it, so he had to silence her. Another version of this says that she learned a lot about Kennedy family secrets, and threatened to leak those to the public. Teamsters president and Mob man Jimmy Hoffa was also involved (Kennedy was pursuing charges against Hoffa). This theory was first proposed by some very anti-Kennedy sources, who thought that Robert and John were communist spies.

She was indirectly killed by Robert Kennedy and his accomplices. Once again, the idea was that they had had an affair and she threatened to expose it, so Kennedy deliberately encouraged her drug addiction, in the hope that she would accidentally overdose. And this is exactly what happened. To make things even more sinister, she didn't die at home, but in an ambulance on the way to a hospital, and Kennedy changed the story to say that she was found dead.

She was murdered by the CIA. Or maybe the FBI. It had to do with a feud between the CIA and President John F. Kennedy (since she was also having an affair with him), and they had her killed in revenge for what they saw as his botching of key presidential policies.

She was killed by the Mafia as a warning. Again, going back to the Robert Kennedy affair, this theory states that she was murdered by the Mafia as a warning to him to back off from investigating them and trying to prosecute key Mob bosses.

John F. Kennedy had her murdered. This is pretty much the same idea as with his brother Robert. She was having an affair with John as well, and he decided to have her silenced when she threatened to expose it, which would probably have resulted in him having to resign. Of course, if he'd resigned then, he might never have been assassinated.

She was murdered because was going to expose the truth about UFOs. Sure, why not?

DID ELVIS PRESLEY FAKE HIS OWN DEATH?

ELVIS PRESLEY WAS THE "KING OF ROCK 'N' ROLL," a worldwide icon beloved by millions. But by the mid-1970s, he was under increasing pressure and was struggling with drug addiction and the stress of the celebrity lifestyle. Even so, his death on August 16, 1977, shocked his fans and the world. While there had been whispers about his troubles, the news that he died was astonishing and horrible to many people. But what caused his death? Here is where things get interesting and lead to many conspiracy theories.

Almost immediately, it was announced that Elvis had died of a heart attack. The medical examiner even assured everyone that drugs had played no part in Elvis's death. But this hasty decision didn't feel right to a lot of people, especially other doctors and medical professionals. A report released a few months later suggested that he might have had as many as fourteen different prescription drugs in his system at the time of his death, which almost certainly meant that he had died of an overdose, or a toxic combination of them. In fact, his doctor, George Nichopoulos, was found to have prescribed him over 10,000 (!) doses of various medications in 1977 alone! Nichopoulos went on trial in 1981, and was amazingly found not guilty of causing Elvis's death (though he later lost his medical license), but a lot of questions remained, and some people started to suspect a cover-up. Other reports suggested that Elvis was sick with diabetes, glaucoma, and constipation (brought on from abusing so many prescription drugs). One report even suggested that he had strained so hard on the toilet that he gave himself a heart attack, which is not impossible, strange as it sounds.

Some began to suspect that the King, simply tired of being a star and wanting out, faked his own death and disappeared to start a new life in hiding. Another, seemingly well-researched theory says that he went into witness protection to escape the Mafia, and had been secretly working with the FBI to help bring down mobsters. Researcher Gail Brewer-Giorgio wrote a book in 1988, entitled *Is Elvis Alive?* In it, she revealed what she claimed was evidence in FBI documents that Elvis had been secretly working with the FBI to bring down a racketeering group called "The Fraternity."

There were reports of a mysterious black helicopter landing at his home, Graceland, in the hours before his body was found and recovered. It seems that a former employee of Elvis's saw him board this helicopter, and even produced photographs to prove it. The existence of this helicopter has never been proven. Some think that he was flown to Bermuda to hide out.

There were also reports of his so-called body looking odd, as if the face were covered in wax or makeup, and many pointed out that the middle name on his tombstone is misspelled as "Aaron" rather than "Aron," though it seems that he did use this spelling too, especially later in life. And, of course, there have been so many "sightings" of Elvis over the years that they have become joke stories for tabloids. Did Elvis Presley die on that August day? Probably, but the idea that he faked his own death is not as crazy as it might at first seem!

DID JIM MORRISON DIE AS CLAIMED, OR DID HE DIE AT ALL?

A YOUNG ROCK ICON and lead singer for The Doors, Jim Morrison died in Paris on July 3, 1971, at the age of twenty-seven. His legions of fans were shocked, and it brought to an end a career that many thought was just beginning. His girlfriend, Pamela Courson, found him dead in the bathtub of their apartment. The official cause of death was listed as heart failure. But almost immediately, many felt that something was not right about the story.

The first problem was that no autopsy was performed, so people only had Courson's word that she'd found him in the bathtub. She died three years later of a heroin overdose, so she took the truth to the grave with her. But it seems that she might have been hiding something.

Some credible witnesses have said that Morrison actually died at a night-club, Rock'n'Roll Circus. He overdosed on heroin, and when people failed to revive him, he was taken to his home and dumped in his own bathtub. Courson either went along with this, or was warned to stay silent. Versions of this story also speculate that he might have lived for a few days before Courson reported his death. The nightclub never said anything about what happened, because they wanted to avoid a scandal and a possible investigation into all of the drug dealing and taking that went on there. Singer Marianne Faithfull said that it was her boyfriend, "a drug dealer to the stars" named Jean de Breteuil, who gave Morrison the heroin that killed him, and that it was an accidental overdose.

There were other theories, of course. One was that the CIA or the American military targeted Morrison. His father, George Morrison, was an important rear admiral in the navy, and many think that it was a source of embarrassment to him that his son was a wildly popular face for the counterculture movement, a poet and musician whose bohe-mian lifestyle was so at odds with his family. Given that the CIA wanted to eliminate certain icons of the movement, some speculate that they assassinated him by making it look like a heroin overdose, and then threated his girlfriend to keep quiet. This was also why no autopsy was ever performed. Whether or not his father approved of his son's murder is unknown.

There were possibilities, including one proposed by The Doors keyboardist Ray Manzarek.

He said that Morrison was weary of the rock-and-roll lifestyle and the fame, and might have wanted to disappear. If so, he faked his own death, which explained the conflicting reports about what had happened to him. Indeed, in 2016, there were rumors on the internet that Morrison was alive and well, and living in Oregon under the name of William Loyer. Some people claimed that Loyer, an old man, bore a resemblance to what Morrison would look like as an older man. But many are not convinced and think it's all absurd. Still, the fact that Loyer was said to work at the Jim Morrison Sanctuary Ranch just made the case all the more suspicious.

It seems there are still questions about what happened in the days before and after Morrison's death, and many are convinced that the whole story has not yet been told.

THE DEATH OF KURT COBAIN: SUICIDE OR MURDER?

GRUNGE ROCKER KURT COBAIN shocked the music world when he died on April 5, 1994 (though his body would not be discovered until April 8). He was found with a shotgun in his lap, a visible wound to the head, and a suicide note. It seemed to be a tragic end to someone who was known to have struggled with drug addiction and might have been reeling from the pressure of stardom that his band, Nirvana, had brought him. The official police ruling was that it was a suicide. But quite a few people believed there was more to the story, and that he might have actually been murdered, with the killing then made to look like a suicide.

The most vocal of these theorists is private investigator Tom Grant, a former L.A. County deputy sheriff. Grant has made extensive investigations into the case, and has concluded that Cobain's wife, Courtney Love, was probably behind a plot to murder him and cover it up. Grant had originally been hired by Love to investigate why Cobain had gone missing in the days before he died, but he ended up becoming convinced that she was involved.

He found her behavior to be strange; she was said to have filed a missing person report under the name of Wendy O'Connor, who was Cobain's mother. Cobain's lawyer confirmed that there was tension between Cobain and Love, and that Cobain had asked him to remove all mention of Love from his will a few weeks before he died. Grant believed that he intended to divorce her and leave her nothing in the settlement.

Grant also claimed that Cobain had taken an enormous amount of heroin, about three times a lethal dose, and that there was no way that anyone with that amount of the drug in their system could have lifted a gun and shot themselves in the mouth. Further, he insisted that the so-called suicide note was inconsistent. The top part was written by Cobain, and seemed to be more of an announcement of retirement, while the bottom part had different handwriting and mentions his daughter.

A shock-rock singer named Eldon Hoke claimed in 1997 that Love had offered him $50,000 to kill Cobain, but he arranged for someone else to commit the crime. Of course, there was no way to substantiate his claims, but it's worth noting that only a few days after making the claim in an interview, he was killed when he was hit by a train. There were apparently no witnesses.

The theory that Cobain was murdered was believed by some, including members of his own family, while more people accepted that he was struggling with addiction and bipolar disorder and took his own life. His mother confirmed that the note that Grant said was written by two different people could indeed have been written entirely by Cobain, for example. Additional forensic investigations have concluded that the angle of the gunshot wound was consistent with suicide.

But questions remain, and despite the fact that the official report has labeled Cobain's death a suicide, many believe that it was a murder, perhaps orchestrated by his wife to ensure that she would inherit his money.

PRINCESS DIANA WAS MURDERED

THE WORLD WAS SHOCKED by the untimely death of Princess Diana in a car accident in a Paris tunnel on August 31, 1997. Diana was a beloved public figure, but also a controversial one. Her troubled relationship with Prince Charles and the British royal family was the stuff of regular UK tabloid headlines. The official report was that Diana and her partner, Dodi Fayed, were being driven in a car that sped up to avoid the paparazzi that were pursuing them. The driver of the car, Henri Paul (head of security at the Ritz Hotel in Paris), had been drinking and lost control, slamming into the tunnel wall. He, Diana, and Dodi were all killed. In the aftermath of the crash, there was an outpouring of grief all over the world, but many felt that members of the royal family were a bit too reserved. They were obviously unhappy with Diana, but maybe this tragedy was just what they needed? Maybe it was even something they planned?

Almost immediately, Dodi's father, Mohamed Al-Fayed, began declaring that his son and Diana had been murdered. Soon, others found details about the story that didn't seem to add up, and they began to question the official explanation. Here are some of the main conspiracy theories about that tragic night, and the events that led up to it:

Diana's death would make it easier for Prince Charles to remarry. While they were already divorced, there were still questions about various legal issues, titles, inheritance, and so on. With Diana out of the picture, Charles could simply marry again and not have to worry. But Charles could have married again, in any case. There was a debate about whether a divorced man could be king, but given that the founder of the Church of England, Henry VIII, had divorced his wife and set up the Church, this wouldn't have been much of an issue.

Diana was pregnant. The theory is that Diana was pregnant and Dodi was the father. The royal family would never have allowed an Egyptian Muslim man to father a child with a member of the royal family, so she was killed to avoid that scandal. But Diana's autopsy revealed no signs of her being pregnant at the time. Skeptics think that report was falsified.

Diana worried that she would be killed. This was actually true. In a letter from the mid-1990s held by her butler, Paul Burrell, she expressed concern that she might die as a result of her car being sabotaged. She'd had car troubles before and thought that someone might have tampered with it.

Bright lights flashing in the tunnel. Three different eyewitnesses claimed to have seen a bright light flash before the crash. The theory is that this flashing may have been deliberately set off to blind the driver, causing him to crash the car. But these stories contradicted each other, and other witnesses in the tunnel made no mention of a flash. The flash(es) might have been from paparazzi cameras.

The car itself was sabotaged. As Diana had feared, someone could have tampered with the car so that it would fail and crash. But investigations of the car found nothing wrong with it. Witnesses didn't report it acting in an unusual way beforehand, e.g., wobbling or weaving on the road, giving off smoke, or any other issues.

A detailed investigation, Operation Paget, was launched to look into all of these and dozens of other theories, but was unable to confirm any of them. And questions still remain.

PRINCE CHARLES IS A VAMPIRE

THE BRITISH ROYAL FAMILY is both loved and hated, and famous throughout the world. They are still a huge draw for tourists to the UK, and even those who would love to see the royals abolished and Britain become a republic have to admit that the tourist money and industry is very profitable. But it's only natural that a family that is so liked and loathed will have countless stories told about them, rumors spread, lies made up, and everything else. From Diana's alleged murder to Queen Elizabeth II's unusual diet (see the next entry), there is no shortage of good royal yarns to keep people interested. One of the weirder (and most unlikely) ones is that Prince Charles is actually a vampire!

Okay, probably not too many people take this seriously, but it is at least based on something that is a verifiable fact. Charles traces some of his ancestry back to the infamous Vlad the Impaler, the fifteenth-century tyrant who ruled Wallachia (in modern Romania) at various times. Vlad's family name was, of course, Dracula, and Irish novelist Bram Stoker used Vlad's name and parts of his life as inspiration for the most famous fictional vampire of all.

Vlad was certainly a brutal and cruel man. He was called "the Impaler" for a good reason: one of his preferred methods of execution was to impale his victims on long wooden stakes, a horrible fate that would cause them to die slowly over hours, even days. He was said to have committed all kinds of other atrocities and tortures, such that his own people were terrified of him. But he was also an effective military commander, and succeeded at stopping the advancement of the Ottoman Turks into his country for several years.

So, when people heard that Charles is distantly related to Vlad, some just assumed this must be "proof" that Charles is a vampire from a long line of vampires. Except that, while Vlad was a sadistic and evil monster, there's no evidence that he ever drank blood, no matter what many horror writers like to claim. Still, legends persisted that after his death, he rose from the grave, and it was said that when his coffin was opened some years after he died, his body was not in it. But folktales have nothing to do with the modern royal family, so this conspiracy theory can confidently be set aside.

One curious truth in all of this is that some lines of various royal families are more prone to a disease called porphyria, which is a kind of iron deficiency that causes its sufferers to be sensitive to sunlight. It's been suggested that centuries ago, those who had this disease might have been viewed with suspicion and fear by others. If they feared sunlight, what else did they do? And did some of them turn to consuming blood because their bodies craved more iron?

QUEEN ELIZABETH II
IS A CANNIBAL

QUEEN ELIZABETH II OF ENGLAND is probably the best-known and even most loved monarch in the world. She has been England's queen since 1953, and is famed for her colorful outfits, small stature, and beloved corgi dogs. Whether people love her or loathe her, she is still a force to be reckoned with, even if she does present as a quiet and reserved person. But could a horrible monster be lurking under that calm exterior? Some conspiracy theorists think so.

According to one report, a serviceman was once given clearance in Windsor Castle to check on some electrical problems. He was accompanied by three constables (police), who waited in another room while he went to work. Sure enough, he found various problems, especially with an old freezer. When he opened it up, he saw strips of what looked like bacon laid out in clear plastic wrap. But there was something odd about them, something wrong. Sensing that this was very off, he fetched the police, who came back with him, noting that he seemed quite shaken.

He opened the freezer again and they set about exploring it. They found what they at first thought were pig parts, but which they quickly realized were actually human. In addition to those strips of flesh, they were said to have found a frozen arm, part of a leg, and part of a man's chest. Apparently, they also found some other parts that they didn't want to talk about. These parts seemed to be kept for eating, as there was other food in the freezer, too.

Of course, the police officers thought that they should open up a crime report, try to check DNA, and so on, but there was a problem: the monarchy has special privileges under British law and cannot be prosecuted. In other words, if they wanted to, kings and queens could get away with anything. So, the officers were forced to shut up about it, and to only discuss it when they could remain anonymous.

Other reports have claimed that the queen howls and acts crazy when in private, that she has sharp teeth that are hidden under false ones, and that she has far more energy than someone her age should have; eating human flesh is rumored to give one a long life.

All of this sounds horrible and makes for a very unsettling story, but, as you might guess, there's a problem: there is no proof that the freezer story ever actually happened. As is so often the case with these kinds of reports, it's an urban legend, something told by a "friend of a friend" and passed on as true. Anyone can make up any story and claim that it really happened, and it will eventually be impossible to prove one way or the other. That's how many good urban legends and conspiracy theories start.

So without any more evidence, we can take this story and this outrageous claim with a very big grain of salt. It's highly likely that this bizarre tale is simply a load of nonsense intended to slander a woman whom many people love, but also whom many people don't.

KEANU REEVES IS IMMORTAL

OKAY, THIS ENTRY IS SILLY, and a bit of fun, but it has attracted a lot of interest over the last several years, and even some devoted believers. What mostly started as a joke has become a fun pastime for some, as they delve into history looking for images of men from previous centu-

ries who bear a resemblance to actor Keanu Reeves. Surprisingly, they've come up with a few. And the website keanuisimmortal.com has the "proof." The site, created by a man known only as Davide, posts images of men from the past who look like Reeves, as well as photos of him from the 1990s to the present that show him seemingly not aging at all. He definitely looks good for his age!

Davide says that he started the website after seeing a painting of French actor and medical doctor Paul Mounet (1847–1922) as a young man. Several other people pointed out that he bears a similarity to Reeves. Rumors began to circulate that Mounet's body was never found after he supposedly died. Other researchers found a striking similarity between Reeves and a painting said to be a self-portrait of a sixteenth-century Italian artist named Parmigianino, further showing that whoever Reeves really is simply changes occupations every seven decades or so, and assumes a new identity. Some have speculated that he might have even been the Emperor Charlemagne (who "died" in the year 814).

And so a conspiracy site was born! Admittedly, the site is small and definitely tongue-in-cheek, but believers like to point out that when Reeves has been asked about this whole business, he doesn't outright deny it. And why would he? It's fun, it gets people talking, and who wouldn't like to be thought of as immortal?

If he is immortal, what is he? Some have suspected that he might be a vampire, but he seems too kind and compassionate for that. Also, he's out in the daylight, a lot. So, some kind of other being, then? Others have speculated that he might not be immortal, but rather a time traveler from some unknown future age. Films like the *Bill & Ted* and *Matrix* series provide clues about his true identity, apparently.

Of course, this is all nonsense, but in the realm of conspiracy theories, it's pretty harmless and a fun diversion from some of the darker beliefs, especially the ones that might actually do some damage. Is Keanu Reeves immortal? We can only hope. And if not, he should be.

BRITNEY SPEARS IS A CLONE

BRITNEY SPEARS HAS BEEN in the news on many occasions over the past two decades, and a lot of that news has been negative or seeking to dig up something scandalous about her. It's an unfortunate fact that some celebrities and famous artists are just going to be hounded by reporters, paparazzi, bloggers, and anyone else looking for a story to elevate themselves. Spears is no stranger to these, but one of the weirder conspiracy theories about her is that she's not the original Britney. No, the current version is a clone, or maybe a clone of a clone.

This strange tale dates to the early days of her rising stardom. In June 2001, two DJs on a radio station in San Jose, California, reported that Spears and her then boyfriend, Justin Timberlake, were involved in an automobile accident in Los Angeles that killed them both. Spears was allegedly driving drunk at over a hundred miles an hour, and an alcohol flask had been found at the site of the wreckage.

Naturally, fans of both stars panicked, and local police stations and hospitals were flooded with calls, not only from those upset fans, but also reporters. Though major news outlets picked up the story, it prompted spokespeople for both Spears and Timberlake to issue statements saying that the two were fine, and it was all a mistaken rumor. This satisfied some, but not all, and some people demanded further proof. It turned out that the DJs in question had been in trouble before for making controversial on-air statements, and it seems that this was nothing more than a twisted and cruel practical joke.

Spears and Timberlake were alive and well, and subsequent appearances proved that it had all been false. Except, not everyone was convinced. By then, the story had spread far enough that some conspiracy theorists began to see something more secretive. The two really were in an accident, they claimed, and the Britney and Justin that people were seeing? Those were clones. Yes, clones. Spear's record label had recognized her value and had prepared a selection of clone bodies to use when needed. Spear's clean image at the time had to be preserved, so the idea that she'd been driving while drunk or under the influence of drugs and had decapitated herself would not sit well with her legions of fans. Cloned Britneys were the perfect solution!

THE BIG BOOK OF CONSPIRACY THEORIES

As for Timberlake? Well, some believed that he had actually survived, but was badly burned and could no longer go out in public, so a clone of him was produced too. It makes for a perfect conspiracy, except for the fact that cloning technology like that doesn't exist. But never let the facts get in the way of a good story! And the story was good enough that it still has some believers to this day.

BOB MARLEY WAS MURDERED BY THE CIA

BOB MARLEY, THE REGGAE ICON, died on May 11, 1981. The cause of death was listed as a melanoma that had spread to his brain. But given his position in the music scene, his political stances, and past run-ins with authority, some people suspected there was more to the story than that. There had been an attempt on his life before his cancer diagnosis; he was shot and wounded at his home in 1976, possibly for supporting Jamaican Prime Minister Michael Manley (who was sympathetic to Castro and Cuba), so it's possible that Marley had stirred up some anger and hatred in certain groups.

The most common conspiracy theory is that he was murdered by the CIA, because his political activities and the movement he was starting were at odds with their objectives in various places around the world. A video on YouTube shows a photo of an elderly man named Bill Oxley, who claims to be an ex–CIA agent. He also says that he killed Marley, and that he was responsible for seventeen assassinations around the world between the mid-1970s and the mid-1980s. In an incredible deathbed confession, Oxley says that he was part of a team that went after activists and political dissidents, as well as "scientists, medical researchers, artists, and musicians whose ideas and influence represented a threat to the interests of the United States." Bob Marley, he says, "was succeeding in creating a revolution that used music as a more powerful tool than bullets and bombs."

And so, Marley had to be eliminated. The agency had tried to warn him off his path in the past, including firing shots at his home. When Marley persisted, the decision was made to take him out. Oxley (or in some versions, his son), posing as a photographer for *The New York Times*, went to visit Marley at a mountain retreat in 1976, and offered him a gift of some new shoes. When Marley put them on, he cried out in pain, because something had stuck him in the toe. And that sealed his fate. The copper wire in the shoe was contaminated with bacteria and cancer viruses, which, over time, spread and killed him.

It was a stunning admission that, for many conspiracy theorists, was a smoking gun which not only proved that Marley had been murdered, but that the CIA routinely engaged in such practices when it needed certain people removed. The problem was, the video has been examined and determined to be a fake, or questionable at best. There is no record of a "Bill Oxley" ever having worked for the Agency, and the methods he described to kill Marley would have been difficult to achieve at best. Why, if the CIA wanted Marley eliminated, would it choose a method of assassination that would take over four years to work? Still, believers are not convinced, and think that there is much more to the story of Marley's death than has been fully revealed.

MICHAEL JACKSON CONSPIRACY THEORIES

THE DEATH OF POP ICON Michael Jackson on June 25, 2009, left millions of fans stricken with grief. It seemed inconceivable that a singer and dancer that so many had grown up with, who had produced megahits like *Thriller*, could suddenly be gone. Officially, the cause of death was listed as a heart attack, brought about by an overdose of propofol, a medication used in administering anesthesia. It and other medications were given to him to help him sleep, but he received too much, and doctors couldn't revive him at a hospital. That's the story

SED ARX TUTA EST MORTIS AB IMPERIO. SIVE SUMUS

FORTE LOCUS DABITUR CONTRA OMNIA CÆTERA TUTUS: NULLA

SCEPTRO INSIGNES, SIVE ARVA LIGONE PERFODIMUS, ΘΑΝΑΤΩ, ΠΑΝΤΕΣ ΟΦΕΙΛΟΜΕΘΑ.

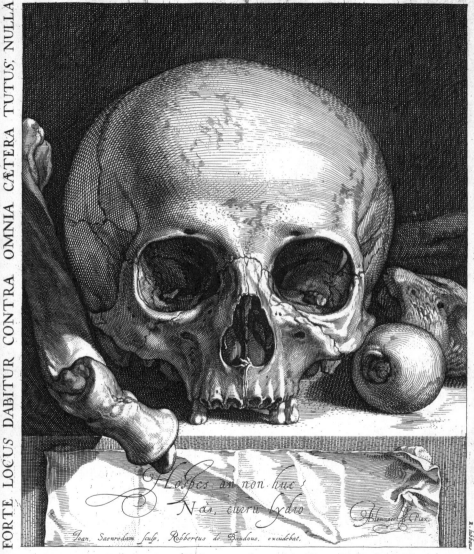

Hospes an non huc!
Nας, ευαρυ ςyδiω

Ioan. Saenredam sculp. Robbertus de Baudous. excudebat.

(ἔκοςος) ΘΝΑΤΑ΄ ΜΕΜΝΑΣΘΩ ΓΕΡΙΣ ΤΕ΄ΛΛΩΝ ΜΕΛΗ. Pindarus

told by the mainstream press, anyway. It was a tragic accident that need not have happened. But to many, including some members of Jackson's own family, there was more to the story. Here are some of the most common conspiracy theories circulating out there:

He is still alive. Of course, this theory is the most popular among his hopeful fans. He faked his own death to get away from the extreme pressures of fame and stardom and the toll they were taking on him. An investment banker testified in 2017 that Jackson was also heavily in debt and was trying to get out from under it. There is footage online of a coroner's van (like the one that took Jackson away) pulling into a garage, and a man resembling Jackson being ushered out of it and into a building. Rumors have circulated that the paramedics who rushed to the scene saw that it wasn't Jackson at all, but were made to keep quiet. In 2017, hairdresser Steve Erhardt, a personal friend of Jackson's, made various online posts which teased that Jackson was alive and would soon reveal himself, though nothing came of it. And, of course, there have been countless sightings around the world over the past decade-plus of someone that people think is Jackson.

He was murdered. Paris Jackson, Michael's daughter, flat out told *Rolling Stone* in a 2017 interview: "All arrows point to that. It sounds like a total conspiracy theory and it sounds like bullsh**, but all real fans and everybody in the family know it. It was a setup." La Toya Jackson, Michael's sister, has claimed that more than once, he told her, "I'm going to be murdered for my music publishing catalogue and my estate." She has long insisted that he was afraid there was a conspiracy to kill him, since his music catalogue would be very valuable to whoever was able to obtain the rights.

He killed himself. Some believe that Jackson, facing financial ruin, addiction, and possible consequences for abuse allegations, took his own life. Though his doctor, Conrad Murray, was sentenced to four years (and served two) for involuntary manslaughter in administering lethal doses of medication to him, Murray's own lawyer had argued that Jackson took his own life, deliberately overdosing to escape from the financial and other problems that were closing in on him.

In all likelihood, Jackson died of an accidental overdose, but there are enough alternative theories out there to keep people talking for a long time.

THE DEATH OF BRIAN JONES: ACCIDENT OR MURDER?

BRIAN JONES WAS THE FOUNDER of the Rolling Stones in 1962, and even gave the band its name. He was a central figure in the group in those early days, but gradually his life began to spin out of control, as drug addiction and run-ins with the law caught up with him. The band (including Mick Jagger and Keith Richards) decided in June 1969 to kick him out of his own band. Jones took the news gracefully, and went on to announce to the public that they were parting ways over musical differences (the usual excuse). That might have been the end of it, but just a few weeks later, Jones was found dead at the bottom of the swimming pool at his house. While his girlfriend insisted that he was still alive at the time, he was later pronounced dead at a nearby hospital. The cause of death was listed as "death by misadventure," given the drugs in his system. People assumed that he must have fallen in and drowned. But, of course, almost immediately there were suspicions that there was more to the story, and that the police covered up evidence of murder because they had botched the investigation. So, what happened? Here are some of the popular theories:

Jones was murdered by Frank Thorogood. This has been a top theory for some time. Jones and builder Thorogood had allegedly argued earlier in the day over money that Thorogood felt he was owed. It was said that they got into a scuffle by the pool, and Thorogood even held Jones's head underwater for a time. Later, in 1993, Thorogood allegedly confessed to the band's chauffeur, Tom Keylock. Keylock said Thorogood had made a deathbed confession, but when he went back to learn more, Thorogood had already passed away.

Jones was murdered by Tom Keylock. For some, this confession was a little too convenient, and they suspected that Keylock himself was the murderer, or at least planned it and had someone else carry it out. Keylock was not only the band's driver, he was also a fixer, helping them out of legal troubles, and Jones represented a major problem.

The band ordered Jones to be murdered. Keylock might have orchestrated the murder, but he was ordered to do so by the band, who still saw Jones as a liability. Plus, it was said that he wanted the "Rolling Stones" name back, since he'd come up with it. There were rumors that Keith Richards had argued with Jones earlier in the day, and even threatened him with a knife. He later told Keylock to arrange for Jones to die.

Jones was murdered as a satanic sacrifice. Well, why not? The band had released an album called *Their Satanic Majesties Request*, after all! Some speculated that they went fully in as satanists, and needed a human sacrifice to seal the deal. Who better than their former bandmate?

Jones was murdered by an agent of the royal family. Last but not least, some speculated that Jones had been having an affair with Princess Margaret, and the last thing the royal family wanted was her associating with someone like him!

So, whoever did it, the police messed up, covered it up, and have kept it secret ever since. Despite reviews of the case saying that there is no evidence for anything other than a tragic accident, the rumors still abound.

THE DEATH OF JIMI HENDRIX: OVERDOSE OR MURDER?

LIKE BRIAN JONES, Jimi Hendrix was a 1960s icon who created legendary music, had legions of devoted fans, and then passed away at a young age, seemingly due to a drug overdose. Hendrix was found unresponsive in a London apartment on September 18, 1970. He was taken to a hospital but was pronounced dead there. The music world was in shock that another of its great stars had passed away at such a young age. He expanded ideas of what was possible for the guitar, and would influence generations of guitarists that came after him. But now, he was gone. The cause of death was listed as choking on his own vomit while under the influence of barbiturates to bring on relaxation. Significantly, though, the coroner couldn't determine the exact circumstances by which Hendrix had died, and almost immediately, that set rumormongers and conspiracy theorists to work, and they've been at it ever since. If it wasn't an accident, who or what killed Hendrix? Here are some theories:

His manager murdered him. Hendrix and his manager, Michael Jeffery, had been in conflict for some time. Hendrix was burned out on music and blamed Jeffery for some of his misfortunes. He ended up telling Jeffery that he was going to replace him with a new manager. Jeffery might have had connections with various intelligence agencies, and had allegedly taken out a $2 million insurance policy, should Hendrix die. When he heard that he was going to be replaced, he decided to cash in. He also later allegedly confessed to this while drunk, but he died in 1973, so he took his secrets with him to the grave.

An obsessed ex-girlfriend accidentally killed him. Monika Dannemann, a figure skater and onetime girlfriend of Hendrix, rented the apartment where he was found dead. She was said to be something of a stalker and was terrified that Hendrix was going to leave her. She may have given him the pills without the intention of killing him, but at least incapacitating him until he changed his mind.

The FBI had him murdered. Hendrix tried not to be overly political, even in a politically charged time, but he did make some casual com-

ments in support of the Black Panthers, a group that was under heavy FBI surveillance. Was Hendrix viewed as subversive and dangerous enough to eliminate?

It was an organized crime hit. According to the paramedics who were on the scene, they found evidence that Hendrix had ingested a huge amount of red wine and vomited it back up. The problem was that Hendrix didn't drink red wine. But shoving pills down someone's throat and then forcing them to ingest alcohol was a known Mafia execution technique. Some speculated that it could even have been the Mafia back in New York, who were unhappy with Hendrix's Electric Lady Studios being so close to their Little Italy.

Hendrix's death is still shrouded in mystery. It's entirely possible that he overdosed, or maybe even took his own life, but enough questions remain that the suspicious think there is more to the story than most people realize.

STEVE JOBS IS ALIVE

STEVE JOBS, THE COFOUNDER OF APPLE, was a hugely influential figure in the world of personal computing and beyond. He and cofounder Steve Wozniak launched Apple in the 1970s, and, along with Bill Gates and Microsoft, created a revolution in personal computing that ultimately brought computers into the homes of people all over the world. The introduction of the Apple Macintosh in 1984 changed the world of home computers, but Jobs was forced out of the company the following year. He had the last laugh, though, coming back in 1997 to become the CEO of the company. Apple was in big trouble at that point, and Jobs brought it back from bankruptcy, introducing the innovations that made Apple the star of the computing world over the next fifteen years: sophisticated laptops, the iPad, the iPod, iTunes, the iPhone, and much more. Apple was the coolest company, and everyone wanted to have at least something made by them.

Jobs tragically died of pancreatic cancer on October 5, 2011, at the young age of fifty-six. Many feel that Apple has never been the same without him, and his loss was felt throughout the industry. But some people think he might not have died after all. In 2019, someone posted a photo to Reddit of a man in Egypt, sitting in a plastic chair and seen in profile, noting that the man bore an amazing resemblance to Steve Jobs. The individual does indeed bear a striking resemblance to Apple's star, and the post received countless replies both in favor of and against the idea.

Those in favor say that the resemblance is rather uncanny, and even the man's hand held up to his chin and mouth is a gesture that Jobs used to do frequently. The hair and thin beard are also almost identical, and he seems to be wearing the same kind of glasses that Jobs did. Could Jobs have faked his death to get away from an industry that he was increasingly frustrated with? He was such an important figure in computing, with all eyes on him for whatever Apple would announce next. He might have simply wanted to get away and be done with it all.

Those against the idea say that it's ludicrous and disrespectful to the man and his family. They point out that Jobs was Syrian, so finding a man in Egypt with similar facial features is not at all unlikely. One astute observer pointed out that the man in the photo, though balding, has more hair than Jobs did at the time of his death, so unless he discovered a way to grow it back, it can't be the same man. Also, some joked, the man is wearing an analog watch, when Jobs surely would be wearing an Apple Watch!

Also, many argued there is no way that Jobs would simply have walked away from Apple and pretended to be dead; he wouldn't have let the company out of his control, no matter what kind of a break he might have needed. In the end, this is almost certainly just a look-alike from a similar region of the world. It's said that we all have at least one doppelgänger out there, if not more, so we can safely assume this is one of Jobs's.

AVRIL LAVIGNE IS DEAD AND HAS BEEN REPLACED BY A LOOK-ALIKE

AVRIL LAVIGNE HAS BEEN a popular pop-punk rock musician since the early 2000s. She's also an actress and charity activist with a huge following around the world. Except that some people think it's all a lie. Oh, to be sure, the person in question is quite popular—it's just not Avril Lavigne. The real Lavigne died right at the start of her career, they say, and a look-alike has been impersonating her ever since.

The young Canadian musician was an up-and-comer in 2002, you see, and had everything before her. But she was troubled and reclusive, so she ended up hiring a body double named Melissa Vandella to pretend to be her and distract the media and the paparazzi. This worked fine for the first year or so of her career, but trouble was brewing. She was unable to handle the pressures of fame, and when her grandfather died, it sent her spiraling into depression. She took her own life in late 2003. Her record label and managers were shocked, but decided that they needed to keep the story hidden. They asked Vandella to step in and pretend to be Lavigne, to keep the money from her success rolling in. Vandella agreed, and she's been doing it ever since.

People who believe this conspiracy theory point out a number of supposed discrepancies in the photos of the "real" Avril from 2003 and earlier, and those of her supposed replacement afterward. They have pointed out apparent differences in facial structure, blemishes, and other signs to prove that the person who is performing now is not the original Avril Lavigne.

Others say that her fashion choices were very different after that year, and even her handwriting looks different now.

Believers think that several of her songs have hidden meanings and messages in them that indicate that this is not the real singer-songwriter. There are some who even believe that Lavigne is actually alive, but decided to retire due to stress and depression, and worked out a deal with her record label and Vandella to let the replacement go on and pretend to be her. And, most telling of all, a photo shoot of Avril with the name "Melissa" written on her hand must surely be proof that this is an impostor, right?

Lavigne denied being dead in 2017, and did so again in a radio interview in 2018, when she said, "Some people think that I'm not the real me, which is so weird! Like, why would they even think that?" Believers in the conspiracy theory were quick to point out that this was not a direct denial, even though she'd denied it a year earlier. In 2019, she shot back at the theory, calling it a "dumb internet rumor."

But the idea caught on and is still bandied about on the internet in various places. People who really believe she's long dead won't let go of that belief, and will continue to look for proof.

EMINEM IS DEAD AND HAS BEEN REPLACED BY A CLONE

MARSHALL BRUCE MATHERS III, aka Eminem, is one of the most successful rap artists in music history. He has sold over 200 million records and is instantly recognizable and controversial for his song lyrics, and for his role as a white rapper. The pressures of fame and fortune began to weigh on him, as they often do for those who are young and unprepared, and he resorted to using prescription drugs to numb the pain. Throughout the 2000s, he struggled with addiction, finally overdosing in late 2007, and nearly dying. After a personal struggle, he fought back and was able to get clean. During this time, he took a hiatus from music and performing, returning with new material in 2009 and resuming his career, now drug free.

At least, that's what "they" want you to believe. According to some, the real Eminem died in 2005 or 2006. The circumstances surrounding his death are not clear, but some say that he died of an overdose, while others say that he was high and died in an automobile accident. Others put a darker spin on it. They say that he was approached by members of the

THE BIG BOOK OF CONSPIRACY THEORIES

Illuminati, who wanted him to join their ranks, since he was unusual and influential. But he resisted their invitations, their lure, and so he was murdered for it. Apparently, an offer from the Illuminati is one that you can't refuse. They made his death look like a suicide or an accident, because that's what they do, of course.

In any case, Eminem was dead, and his record label and management were scrambling to find a way to continue to capitalize on his name and fame. And they found it. The same Illuminati that murdered him also took DNA and bone samples and made a clone. They offered this clone up as a substitute—one who would be more controllable, and could still be useful to them. All of this coincided with his overdose, rehab, and hiatus, so those stories provided the perfect cover. When he reemerged in 2009, fans would be none the wiser.

Except some saw through the deception, of course. They noticed changes in his lyrical content, his attitude, and even his appearance. During a 2013 BBC interview, near the end, he stops and stares at the camera in an awkward silence for about fifteen seconds before returning to the interviewer. Some see this "glitch" as proof of external control. Obviously, the cloning wasn't perfect, and if the Illuminati were now controlling this fake, they could also control the messaging and his behavior. It was the only answer!

Except that it's not, of course. People go through tough times in their life. They may change their views and their appearance, and substances can take their toll. It seems far more likely that this is the explanation for any supposed changes in Eminem's music and behavior, rather than that an impostor was cloned by a secret society from a dead rapper's bones!

RECORD BACKMASKING

BACK IN THE GOOD OLD DAYS (which are now the new days again) of vinyl records, an interesting accusation came up. Coinciding with the "satanic panic" (see the Secret Societies chapter), some people starting accusing music artists, especially rock groups, of hiding satanic messages in their music by a process known as "backmasking." They would record a message that would be mixed into the song backward, so it could only be heard when played backward. And those messages were almost always of an occult and evil nature.

Now the truth is, backmasking really is a thing. It's entirely possible to record something and fold it into the master recording backward, so that it's unnoticeable when the song is playing. And none other than the Beatles tossed a little backward recording onto their *Revolver* album in 1966. This set off a storm of controversy after some believed that Paul McCartney had died (see the next entry), and the Beatles were leaving clues to his death as hidden backward messages on later albums.

Of course, it didn't take too long for some to start seeing that back-masking would be the perfect way to place hidden satanic messages that revealed a band's true intentions. In 1982, a televangelist named Paul Crouch accused Led Zeppelin of planting a long, hidden message in their song "Stairway to Heaven." He said that if you listen to a certain portion of it backward, the vocals actually say: "Here's to my sweet Satan/The one whose little path would make me sad, whose power is Satan/He will give those with him 666/There was a little toolshed where he made us suffer, sad Satan."

That's pretty specific and kind of bizarre. People who listened to it had to strain hard to get what Crouch was saying. Robert Plant, the band's vocalist, weighed in on the controversy and said, "Who on Earth would have ever thought of doing that? You've got to have a lot of time on your hands to even consider that people would do that."

And most agreed. But that didn't stop the conspiracy theorists from taking the idea and running with it. With the popularity of bands like Black Sabbath, Judas Priest, and more, it wasn't long before accusations were flying, Salem witch hunt–style, that rock bands were leading young ones into satanic temptation. The fact that no one could hear these messages without equipment to play records or tapes backward was somehow lost on them. And, of course, the 1980s saw a rise in openly satanic-themed metal bands (such as Venom and Mercyful Fate, and then the Nordic black metal bands of the 1990s) that said everything forward anyway, so what would have been the point of backmasking?

Scientists and psychologists say that the act of hearing words in a backward recording is not unlike seeing faces in clouds or foliage. The mind wants to organize things into recognizable patterns, so it's only natural that if one listens to a lot of songs backward, eventually a few sounds here or there will start to make some sense. When we see a face in something where there's not really a face, it's called pareidolia, and that's pretty much what is happening here too. Some bands have indeed added backward messages to their records, especially after the controversy came about, but they did it mainly as a joke.

PAUL MCCARTNEY IS DEAD

THIS CONSPIRACY THEORY goes way back to the 1960s, and there are some who still believe in it, despite all the evidence to the contrary. The story goes that on the rainy night of November 9, 1966, Paul had an argument with the rest of the members of the Beatles at their recording studio, got in his car, and drove off in anger. It was the last thing he would do. For whatever reason, he was in an accident and died, possibly even having been decapitated. This was a horrifying situation, and the rest of the band, knowing what effect this would have on their fans, and also out of guilt, agreed to pretend that it hadn't happened, and to train a look-alike to play the role of Paul. It was said that the British spy service MI5 convinced the band to do this, out of fear that there would be mass suicides among devastated fans if the truth got out.

The impostor was from Scotland and named William Shears Campbell, or sometimes just called Billy Shears. He was about Paul's age and looked very much like him. Since the Beatles had already decided to stop giving live concerts by this time, it would be easier for this fake Paul to pull off the disguise. It turned out that Billy was a very good musician and was able to play the role perfectly, but the other three band members started feeling guilty about this con and decided to leave clues in their lyrics and album covers so that clever fans would figure out the truth.

Believers in this conspiracy say that the band backmasked the truth into certain songs. In "Strawberry Fields Forever," some people say they can clearly hear John Lennon saying, "I buried Paul." Lennon admitted to the backmasking (it had become a joke to them by then), but said that his words were "cranberry sauce." Not everyone believed him.

The cover of *Abbey Road* is said to be further proof, with Paul being the only member not wearing shoes as the band crosses the road in its iconic photograph. Lennon on the right is in white, said to be an angel, while Ringo Starr is the next over, and is supposed to be dressed like an undertaker. George Harrison is the gravedigger. Also, left-handed Paul is seen holding a cigarette in his right hand. All of this was the "proof" that conspiracy theorists needed. Stories of McCartney's death actually helped the band sell more albums, so perhaps no one was in a hurry to completely debunk them!

McCartney shot back at these silly rumors, and did a BBC interview about the topic in early 1969. But believers still weren't convinced. He allowed CBS News and *Life* magazine to photograph him at his farm. These images helped to settle some of the rumors, but the story never really went away, and over the years, people would pop up with new "evidence" that Paul really had died. A few years after the whole thing, Paul said in an interview with *Rolling Stone*, "Someone from the office rang me up and said, 'Look, Paul, you're dead.' And I said, 'Oh, I don't agree with that.'"

THE MURDER OF JOHN LENNON

JOHN LENNON WAS MURDERED outside of his New York City apartment building on December 8, 1980, a killing that shocked the music world and beyond. It's said that at least three Beatles fans killed themselves because they were so upset over the news. Lennon's murderer, Mark David Chapman, was a troubled man with a long history of severe mental illness and a desire to kill a celebrity—any celebrity—to make a name for himself. He had been obsessed with the Beatles as a younger man, but came to be angered and repulsed by Lennon's views and perceived lavish lifestyle. What especially angered him was hearing Lennon say (back in 1966) that the Beatles were "more popular than Jesus." This was unforgivable to him.

Chapman came to New York City in December 1980, having obtained a .38 caliber gun, and on December 8, he waited in the cold weather outside the Dakota apartment building where Lennon lived. At 5 p.m., Lennon and Yoko Ono left the building, and Chapman asked him to sign his copy of Lennon's *Double Fantasy* record, which he did. Chapman didn't shoot him then, because he was in awe of actually meeting him. But he waited until Lennon returned that night, at about 10:30. As Lennon passed, Chapman emerged and fired several shots, four of which hit Lennon in the back. He then sat down and waited calmly for the police to arrive. He offered no resistance to arrest, and soon confessed to the crime and decided to plead guilty. Because of his mental state, he was sentenced to twenty years to life. He is still in prison.

All of this was tragic, and seems to be a shocking case of a very disturbed man not getting the help he needed. Chapman himself admitted that he suffered from schizophrenia and paranoia. But for some conspiracy theorists, there is more to the story than that. Some believe that he was conditioned and trained to kill Lennon, while others have suggested that he didn't kill him at all, and that someone else did.

One of the main conspiracy theories is that the FBI and/or the CIA were worried about Lennon's influence on the young. It's not impossible that the FBI in particular was keeping an eye on Lennon during the activist era of the late 1960s and early 1970s; they had monitored Martin Luther

King Jr. and many others. The theory is that, using some form of mind control (such as hypnosis and/or drugs), they took advantage of Chapman's mental issues and programmed him to kill Lennon. A few books have argued that Chapman was "missing" in Chicago in the days before the murder, and that's where his programming was activated. The policeman who interrogated Chapman would later say that he looked "programmed."

Other theories have suggested that the real murderer was the Dakota doorman, who let Chapman take the fall, but the most outlandish theory is that the true murderer was horror novelist Stephen King!

Still, almost everyone agrees that Chapman was the killer, and the evidence supports that he acted alone. But the debate continues.

THE CATCHER IN THE RYE
TRIGGERS ASSASSINATIONS

THE CATCHER IN THE RYE has been a controversial book since it was first published in 1951 (it had been available in serial form before being published as a novel). The story of an alienated teenager who idolizes childhood and sees the adult world as corrupt, it is considered a classic and is one of the most studied and assigned books in American high schools. But because of its language and controversial scenes, it is also one of the most banned books (from 1961 to 1982, it was the most banned book in the United States). Parents and administrators have accused the book of being a communist plot, and even have insisted on firing teachers for assigning it, all of which has made it a rallying cry for defenders of free speech.

But the book has another controversial reputation, at least in some circles. Certain conspiracy theorists believe that the book has coded language and phrases that can be used to trigger some readers to commit

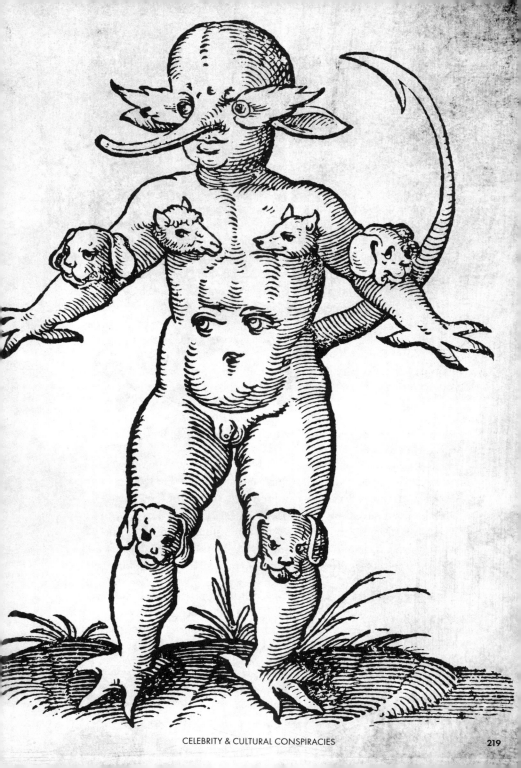

terrible acts, specifically those who have been brainwashed by MK-Ultra or some other government-sponsored program. When one begins to delve into the book's history, it is indeed chilling to learn the number of times that it has shown up in the hands of famous murderers and assassins:

Mark David Chapman. John Lennon's murderer shot the musician and then calmly waited for the police to arrive and arrest him. He passed the time reading *The Catcher in the Rye*. Chapman was obsessed with the book, and had even expressed interest in changing his name to Holden Caulfield, the book's main character.

John W. Hinckley Jr. Hinckley attempted to assassinate President Ronald Reagan on March 31, 1981. While he failed, he offered no resistance to arrest. Police found a copy of *The Catcher in the Rye* in his hotel room. Hinckley was also obsessed with actress Jodie Foster, and allegedly shot Reagan to impress her.

Robert John Bardo. Bardo murdered American model and actress Rebecca Schaeffer on July 18, 1989, and had a copy of the book with him, which he threw away as he fled. He had stalked her for some time.

Lee Harvey Oswald. During a police raid, President Kennedy's assassin was found to have a copy of *The Catcher in the Rye* in his apartment. It was said to be one of his favorite books.

Various other killers are said to have been interested in the book, or fond of it in one way or another, including Jack Ruby (Lee Harvey Oswald's assassin), Charles Manson, James Earl Ray (Martin Luther King Jr.'s murderer), Jonestown founder Jim Jones, Ted Kaczynski (the Unabomber), serial killer Ted Bundy, and Timothy McVeigh (the Oklahoma City bomber), among others. Of course, this might all be hearsay.

Some suspect that the author of *The Catcher in the Rye*, J. D. Salinger, might have inserted various phrases that could be used as triggers for the brainwashed. He was said to have worked in intelligence during World War II, and to have been part of de-Nazification programs. Did he include some of his work in the novel, at the behest of the CIA or

FBI? Was he involved with MK-Ultra? Were these assassins programmed to carry out their crimes by some unknown agency, brainwashing them to be puppets, and to kill at the appointed time? The truth is still being debated.

SUBLIMINAL ADVERTISING

DID YOU KNOW that your mind really isn't your own? That you're not making the choices you think you are? Every time you go to buy something, you've actually been programmed to do it by unseen forces who are manipulating you into buying their products. You've become a slave to their whims, and will obey them when they want you to purchase something, regardless of the consequences to you or your wallet. Sounds pretty sinister and dystopian, but if believers in subliminal advertising are right, it might just be true! But how true is it, really? Let's find out.

Back in 1957, a researcher named James Vicary said that he had conducted a study which proved that people could be influenced to believe and act on certain things—in this case, to buy soda and popcorn at movie theaters. The technique was simple. During the movie or its previews, one or two frames of film would flash a message, such as "buy popcorn," on the screen. It would go by so quickly that viewers' conscious minds wouldn't see it or register it, but on an subconscious level, they would recognize it, and a seed would be planted to make the viewer do what the message requested. Of course, this idea of mind control was dismissed by some, but it outraged a whole lot of people—this was the McCarthy and Cold War era, after all. If secret messages could make you want to buy soda, what else could they do? Could they, for example, turn Americans into traitors and Soviet spies? The practice was banned in several countries by 1958. Vicary later admitted that his study was false, but many didn't think that was the end of the story.

And in truth, it wasn't. Advertisers for companies did start thinking up ways of putting hidden messages into their ads, maybe not as blatant as the idea of flashing a written suggestion in a film, but they were there, nevertheless. Often images would have shapes that could be viewed in more than one way, or when an image was rotated 180 degrees, it might show something very different. This was an actual thing that happened, and companies even admitted it. It was sneaky, but was it an attempt to control buyers? Maybe.

Factors like word choice and placement, design, colors, mood, and a dozen other aspects can all affect how we view a product, a business, a political party, or anything else. Companies spend billions of dollars on advertising, not just to get their messages out, but to make sure that they get the right messages out, done in the right way. It turns out that words, phrases, and images can trigger our reactions, so advertisers want to make sure that they trigger the right kinds of reactions. Now, this doesn't mean that they can "make" us go buy a new car, but we might be more favorable toward that car if it's surrounded by images and phrases that click with us.

Believers in true subliminal advertising will say that it does indeed exist, and is used everywhere to condition people into accepting changes, conditions, hardships, or anything else the entity making the advertising wants. We are more controllable than we think we are, they warn.

The jury is still out on that argument, but there's no doubt that we can be nudged into feeling certain ways, if an ad or a message strikes a chord with us. And tapping into that in just the right way might be a gold mine for the advertisers, and maybe others hidden behind the scenes. . . .

ABOUT THE AUTHOR

It's no conspiracy theory that Tim Rayborn has written a large number of books (more than forty!) and magazine articles (more than thirty!), especially in subjects such as music, the arts, general knowledge, the strange and bizarre, and history. He is conspiring to write more, whether anyone wants him to or not. He lived in England for many years and studied at the University of Leeds, which means he likes to pretend that he knows what he's talking about.

He's also an almost-famous musician who plays dozens of unusual instruments, from all over the world, that most people of have never heard of and usually can't pronounce. He has appeared on more than forty recordings, and his musical wanderings and tours have taken him across the United States all over Europe, to Canada and Australia, and to such romantic locations as Umbrian medieval towns, Marrakesh, Vienna, Renaissance chateaux, medieval churches, and high school gymnasiums.

He currently lives among many books, recordings, and instruments, and a sometimes-demanding cat. He's pretty enthusiastic about good wines and cooking excellent food. Visit timrayborn.com for more on Tim and his work.

ABOUT CIDER MILL PRESS
BOOK PUBLISHERS

Good ideas ripen with time. From seed to harvest, Cider Mill
Press brings fine reading, information, and entertainment
together between the covers of its creatively crafted books.
Our Cider Mill bears fruit twice a year, publishing a new crop
of titles each spring and fall.

"Where Good Books Are Ready for Press"

VISIT US ONLINE AT
cidermillpress.com

OR WRITE TO US AT
PO Box 454
12 Spring St.
Kennebunkport, Maine 04046